BEYOND THE RIVER

Ottoman Transjordan in Original Photographs

BEYOND THE RIVER

Ottoman Transjordan in Original Photographs

Raouf Sa'd Abujaber
and Felicity Cobbing

STACEY
INTERNATIONAL

Beyond the River
Ottoman Transjordan in Original Photographs

published by
Stacey International
128 Kensington Church Street
London W8 4BH
Tel: 020 7221 7166 Fax: 020 7792 9288
E-mail: enquiries@stacey-international.co.uk
Website: www.stacey-international.co.uk

© Stacey International 2005

ISBN: 1900988 8 28

CIP Data: A catalogue record for this book is
available from the British Library

Design: Kitty Carruthers
Printing & Binding: SNP Leefung, China

All rights reserved. No part of this publication may be reproduced,
stored in a retrieval system, or transmitted in any form or by any means,
electronic, mechanical, photocopying, recording, or otherwise,
without the prior permission of the copyright owners.

Title page picture: Photograph of Petra by John Shaw Smith, looking back along the
Royal Tombs to the Urn Tomb, and showing the Palace and Corinthian Tombs.

Contents

Preface by H.R.H. Crown Prince El Hassan bin Talal	7
Acknowledgements	9
Introduction	10
Chapter One Nineteenth Century Travel and Discovery in Transjordan	12
Chapter Two The Land and the People	44
Chapter Three The Rift Valley: Barrier and Gateway	56
Chapter Four The North: Gilead and the Cities of the Decapolis	78
Chapter Five The Middle Range: Ammon	102
Chapter Six The Plateau: Madaba and its Environs	138
Chapter Seven The Southern Range: Moab	152
Chapter Eight The South: Edom and the Nabataean Realm	168
Chapter Nine The Arab Revolt: a New Era	206
Appendix I The Changing Face of Photography & Bibliographies of the Photographers	225
Appendix II List of illustrations	232
Bibliography	237

فوائد الأسفار

تغرب عن الأوطان في طلب العلى
وسافر ففي الأسفار خمس فوائد
تفرج هم واكتساب معيشة
وعلم وآداب وصحبة ماجد

الامام الشافعي – القرن التاسع

The Benefits of Travel

Embark in search of wonders far from home.
Travel and you shall have five rewards –
release from cares, attainment of life's good things,
wide knowledge, art's refinements and good companionship.

Al-Imam Al-Shaffi'i
Ninth Century

Preface

The Hashemite Kingdom of Jordan, Transjordan, or simply Jordan, are all names for a country whose immensely rich and diverse cultural heritage stretches back into the remote reaches of prehistory. Many of Jordan's archaeological sites are everyday names on the itineraries of the modern traveller – Petra, Jerash and Kerak, to name but three. Yet this sense of familiarity has grown up only relatively recently, as indeed has the level of knowledge of the country's past that we now take for granted. It seems now unimaginable that only 200 years ago Jordan was all but unknown to the West, and the exploration of its monuments was in its very infancy. It was also a wild and dangerous place, populated by numerous tribes, not all of whom were particularly receptive to visits by outsiders.

This remarkable work charts the progress of those pioneering and often intrepid travellers, whose adventurous forays into the unknown would lead ultimately to scientific exploration and the recovery of a largely forgotten heritage. Yet this volume goes far beyond a descriptive narrative by illustrating, in a series of extraordinary photographs, the 'coming of age' of Jordan, in the nineteenth century and up to the Arab Revolt.

The book is a true and wonderfully fortuitous collaboration between Raouf Sa'd Abujaber, one of Jordan's most eminent historians, and Felicity Cobbing, Curator of the Palestine Exploration Fund, that most distinguished of learned societies, whose contribution to the scientific study of the Levant is beyond measure. Together, using the Fund's unique collection of photographs, they take us on a fascinating journey in the footsteps of such travellers as Burckhardt and Buckingham. *En route*, we encounter all sorts of other visitors, from amateurs to academics, whose often colourful adventures and exploits amuse, excite and sometimes alarm us.

In the later chapters, the authors introduce us to the early survey teams and excavators (many of whose projects were initiated by the Palestine Exploration Fund) whose dedication and hard work, often in extremely difficult conditions, laid the foundations for a full reconstruction of Jordan's history of civilization.

Raouf Sa'd Abujaber and Felicity Cobbing have produced a work that is an adventure in itself. It is difficult to turn the pages and not be enthralled and captivated by some of the images: is it really possible that within the era of photography Amman has been transformed from the handful of dwellings nestling among the ruins of Roman Philadelphia into the bustling capital city of the Jordanian nation? There are many such pictures which offer a refreshingly new perspective on Jordan and the processes of its emergence as a modern political state. Both authors are to be congratulated for sharing these new insights with us.

El Hassan bin Talal

Acknowledgements

The authors would like to acknowledge the assistance of a number of individuals and institutions. In particular, the support and editorial input of the Chairman of the Palestine Exploration Fund (PEF), Jonathan Tubb, the support of the Executive Committee of the PEF, and the cooperation and assistance of the management and staff at Stacey International Publications.

In addition, the authors would like to thank the following:

In Jordan:
Dr Abdul Karim Gharaybeh, and Dr Ghazi Bisheh, for expert knowledge; the library and curatorial staff at the Department of Antiquities in Amman; Mrs Suhair Shahin, and Mrs Bassima Abujaber-Ghawi for technical support; Mrs Mireille Abujaber for patience and understanding throughout.

In the UK:
Dr Rupert Chapman III of the PEF, for assistance in the library; Graham Edwards of Stacey International, London, and Annabel Lawday for assistance with digitizing the images; Catherine Thomas for assistance with digitizing the images, and general help in the PEF's archives; Brian Greaves for photographic expertise; Dr Archie Walls and Stephen Bank for historical detective work; Paul Smith of Thomas Cook Archives, Peterborough.

Thanks are also due to Mr Ezzat Abdel-Bary and Dr Korayem Al-Daif in Cairo, and Dr Jeff Spurr of the Harvard Fine Arts Library, Boston, USA.

Introduction

Transjordan, the land east of the River Jordan, occupies a unique place in world history, due in the main to its geographical position. It lies on the eastern fringe of the Mediterranean world, and in some western areas enjoys many of the characteristics of climate and agriculture of this most benevolent region. Further to the east, the huge arid zone begins, stretching all the way to the Euphrates River and the region of the Mesopotamian civilizations of antiquity. To the south lies the Arabian Peninsula, another arid region, and to the north, Syria, a land rich in ancient cultures. Transjordan is often considered as part of the 'Holy Land', along with Israel and the Palestinian Territories to the west, and indeed, many important episodes in the biblical accounts are set here. It was from Transjordan, for example, that Moses is said to have seen the 'Promised Land' of Canaan (Deut. 34: 1-12). The significance of the region throughout history, however, extends far beyond that which appears in the pages of the Bible.

Transjordan, as part of the 'Fertile Cresent', in which the first civilizations of the western hemisphere began, occupied a vital position as a crossroads, through which both trade and people were obliged to travel. It was in Transjordan that some of the first experiments in metallurgy were carried out, in the fourth millennium BC the results of which were traded across the Jordan, as well as within Transjordan itself. It was from Transjordan that the Nabataeans conducted their huge trade empire, bringing exotic aromatics and precious goods from as far east as India, and as far south as the Yemen. Through Transjordan, too, came the prophet Mohammad, himself a trader, on his journey from Mecca to Damascus.

Until the start of the twentieth century, the history of Transjordan was not very well known. The weak presence of the aged Ottoman Empire led to a lack of security in the land, which in turn created an unstable climate for foreign travellers. Those who did venture across the River Jordan were, therefore, pioneers in a strange and mysterious land, and most were subjected to continuous hardships, which, in certain cases, cost a few of them their lives. These early travellers were the first to begin to rediscover the past of this fascinating country. From the early 1850s onwards, photography became a valuable addition to the written descriptions and sketches of the country and its people, providing accurate pictorial information, which allowed cultured circles in the outside world the opportunity to see, for the first time, the true grandeur of the cities of the Decapolis, and the splendour of the monuments of Petra, the capital of the Nabataeans.

Since these early days, the historical heritage of Jordan has become far more widely known, due largely to the efforts of the successive Jordanian governments, in collaboration with numerous scholars and experts, both Jordanian and foreign. Many unique sites have been excavated and sometimes restored, attracting huge numbers of tourists to the region.

Yet despite the admirable work that has been conducted in the last decades, it is sometimes illuminating to look back to a time when our current knowledge and understanding of this history had not yet been developed, and for this, the early photographs are invaluable. The monuments and landscapes are seen as yet untouched by archaeologists or experts, and undeveloped by the growing needs of the young nation since 1921. The people of the country, who themselves appear in these images, were themselves part of a culture which would change irretrievably with the development of the modern world. In these terms, the photographs in this volume communicate a sense of pristine reality that is nowadays perhaps less accessible.

This book is not an exhaustive catalogue of photographs of Transjordan, but, rather, has used as its material the photographs in the collections of the Palestine Exploration Fund. As such, some sites are not represented, whilst others are photographed time and time again. In this respect, the collection mirrors the interests of the PEF itself, the explorers who worked for it, and those who donated photographs to it, as much as it does the reality of the land beyond the river that was the focus of their attention.

RSA & FC
May 2005

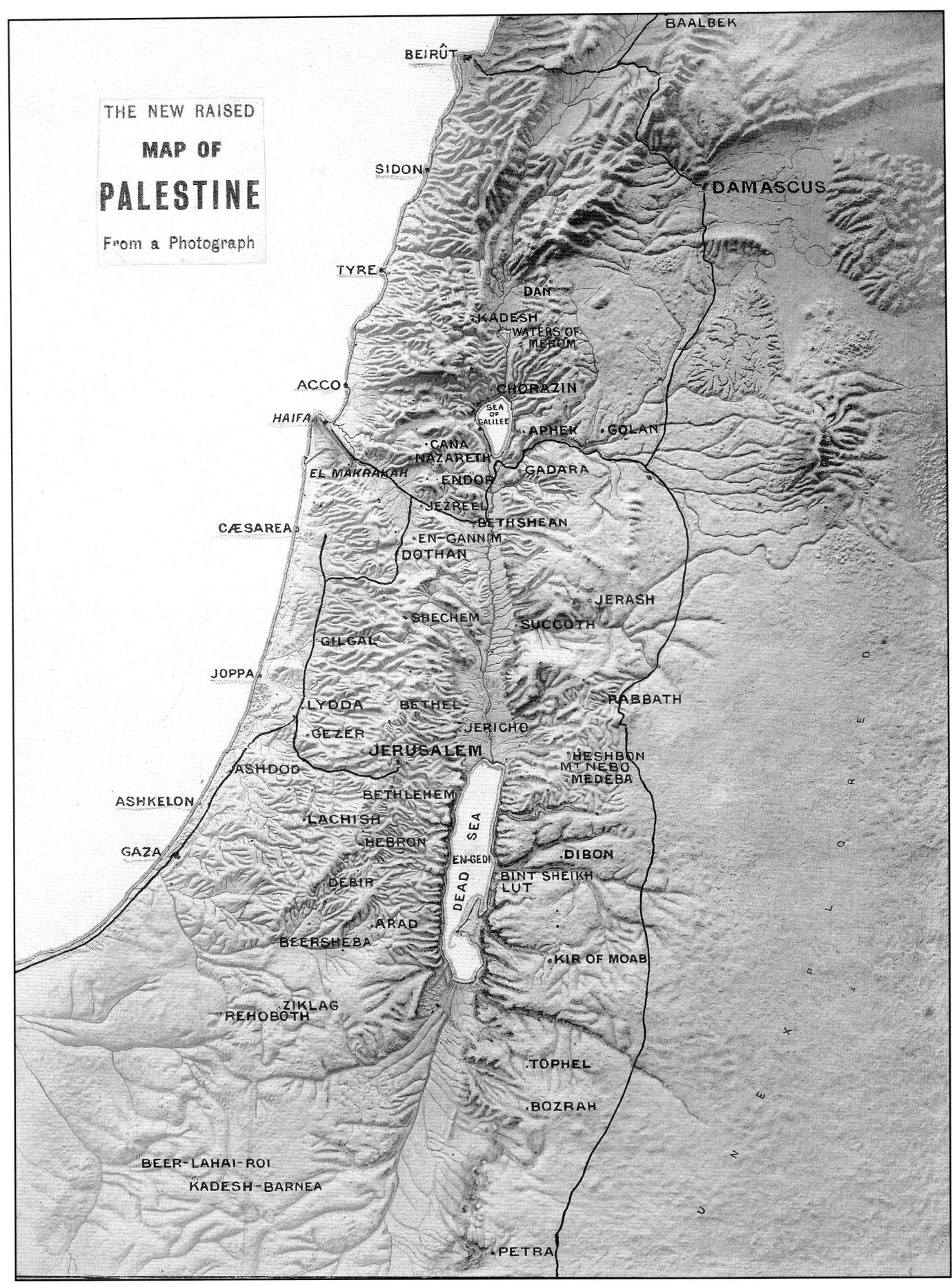

Chapter One

Nineteenth Century Travel and Discovery in Transjordan

Fig.1: Relief model of the PEF's 'Great Map' made by Sergeant George Armstrong, R.E., in 1894. (See Fig.18, p.37.)

Amongst travellers who ventured into Transjordan during the nineteenth century, there seems to have been agreement that it was a wild affair. A seasoned traveller and a leading figure in many ways, Gertrude Lowthian Bell may have been speaking for them all in 1900, when she wrote at the beginning of her famous work, *The Desert and the Sown*, about her most revealing feelings. 'To those bred under an elaborate social order few such moments of exhilaration can come as that which stands at the threshold of wild travel. The gates of the enclosed garden are thrown open, the chain at the entrance of the sanctuary is lowered, with a wary glance to right and left you step forth, and, behold! The immeasurable world. The world of adventure and of enterprise, dark with hurrying storms, glittering in raw sunlight, an unanswered question and an unanswerable doubt hidden in the fold of every hill. Into it you must go alone, separated from the troops of friends that walk the rose alleys, stripped of the purple and fine linen that impede the fighting arm, roofless, defenceless, without possessions' (Bell 1919: 1).

The subject of this book is the area that lies between the Yarmuk River in the north and the Gulf of Aqaba in the south. On its western boundaries are the River Jordan and Wadi Arabah, and in the east the area extends towards the North Arabian and Syrian deserts. Its length from north to south is nearly 400 kilometres and its width varies from 150 kilometres in the narrower parts to over 380 kilometres in the section stretching towards Iraq. The total area is about 96,000 square kilometres of which no less than 80 per cent is steppe and desert. The exact size of the population at the end of the nineteenth century is not known, but a rough estimate puts the figure at around 250,000 people, of

Fig.2: 'Stormy weather on the Sea of Galilee'. Watercolour sketch by J. MacGregor, from his field work book, 1869.

whom nearly 150,000 were city and village dwellers, and the rest, bedouins or nomadic tribes. In 1933, estimates of the British Mandate placed the number of the inhabitants between 300,000 and 350,000, (Luke and Keith-Roach 1934: 435) and today the population exceeds 5.6 million people.

During the Iron Age (c.1150-539 BC), Transjordan was divided into the Kingdoms of Edom, Moab, and Ammon. Part of the wooded hill region of Gilead (which runs roughly along the east bank of the River Jordan from the Yarmuk River in the north to the Arnon River (Mujib) in the south) fell within the kingdom of Ammon, but it does not appear to have had any independent political status, and is quite simply a geographical term (Ottoson 1997: 405-6). Later, in Hellenistic times, Transjordan was one of the territories contested by the descendants of Seleucus and Ptolemy, and under the Romans it formed the outlying province of the Empire south of the Hauran. During these two latter periods the Nabataean Kingdom flourished with its unique capital city at Petra, while Macedonian settlements established after Alexander's conquests developed into other urban centres. Of these, which became better known as the cities of the Decapolis, is the modern capital city of Jordan, Amman, known then as Philadelphia. The prosperity of the Decapolis continued for centuries until its decline during the eighth century AD when the region was rocked by a series of earthquakes.

The Arab conquest in AD 636 saw the area of Palestine and Transjordan divided into two administrative units, Jund el-Urdun in the north and Jund Falastin in the south. The area acquired some importance during the Crusades and the Ayyubid period. In AD 1263, under the Mamluks, the town of Kerak in Moab became the capital of a kingdom, but a few decades after the Ottoman conquest in 1516, the whole area was reduced to the insignificant southern part of the Wilayat, or Governorate of Damascus. During the following 400 years the country suffered the consequences of instability and depopulation, and had it not been for the yearly pilgrimage caravan to Mecca and Medina, which by necessity passed through the region, the whole area could have been forgotten and not even mentioned in government records.

This short historical background is being presented with the purpose of showing how rich the area's history had been until the Ottoman period. No wonder, therefore, travellers in the eighteenth, nineteenth and early twentieth centuries dreamed of visiting the exotic lands across the River Jordan and its fabled ancient sites, in spite of the hardship and danger involved in such trips. Judging by their writings, all of them, without exception, considered themselves well rewarded for their troubles. Visiting east of the Jordan in their times must have felt like visiting the moon in ours.

In this period, European and American travellers had to take into consideration the military and political conditions that prevailed in the Ottoman Empire. The Napoleonic expedition into Egypt and Palestine in 1799 brought about a period of strife and instability that did not provide suitable conditions for travel. After the visits of Volney in the years 1783-1785, we do not come across any important books of travel until the visit of Ulrich Jasper Seetzen in January 1806. Hakim Moussa, as he was known in Transjordan, was the first of a group of illustrious travellers who made their journeys between this time and prior to the Egyptian invasion of Syria in 1831. He was followed by Burckhardt, Irby and Mangles, and Laborde, whose adventures will be covered in due course.

Although German by birth, Seetzen was a councillor to the Embassy of the Emperor of Russia. His book, *Brief Account of the Countries Adjoining the Lake of Tiberias, the Jordan and the Dead Sea*, was published by the Palestine Association of London in 1810. He travelled south from Damascus with one companion and crossed the bridge over Shariat el-Mandhour, better known as the Yarmuk River. He visited Beit Ras, Irbid, and el-Husn, where people advised him to throw aside everything that might tempt the cupidity of the Arabs (meaning the nomadic bedouins) if he wished to continue his journey to the east of the Jordan and the Dead Sea.

Seetzen was struck by the fact that the Balqa region, which commences south of the Zarqa River, formerly so populous and flourishing, was even then changed into a deserted wilderness in which there was only one inhabited town, Salt. In this place he became acquainted with an Arab poet who recited to him a poem in which he invited his people to join the standard of Bonaparte during the French Invasion of Syria. The people of Salt enjoyed some unusual privileges, particularly freedom from every kind of taxation, and they acknowledged no master. Seetzen then visited Amman, which had been destroyed and deserted for many years, followed by the Wadi es-Sir, Hesban, and on to Kerak. He and his companions carried with them a supply of bread as the whole country between Salt and Kerak was uninhabited. There were three inhabited villages in the Kerak area, and seven in the district of Jebbal, in the area of Tafileh. In the district of esh-Sharah there was only one inhabited village, Shobak. Whilst in Kerak, Seetzen inquired about Petra. He was assured it was the distance of only one day's journey away. Unfortunately for him he never saw the legendary city, as he joined a group of Hebron and Bethlehem inhabitants who had brought several hundred sheep from Kerak and were on their return journey around the Dead Sea. They arrived in Jerusalem on Easter Day, 2 April 1806.

Four years later the Swiss traveller, John Lewis Burckhardt, was more successful in this regard. His trips to the Orient were financed and organized by the African Association in London, and were truly groundbreaking in their daring and discovery. Burckhardt was a singularly intrepid and resourceful character. Possessing a good knowledge of Arabic, he assumed the name Sheikh Ibrahim during his journey, a tactic which makes his accounts among the most informative of all travellers to the region. He wrote many books, but those that are of interest for our area are, *Travels in Syria and The Holy Land* (published 1822), *Travels among the Arab Tribes Inhabiting the Countries East of Syria and Palestine* (1825), *Travels in Arabia* (1829), *and Notes on the Bedouins and the Wahabys* (1830). During the summer of 1812 he embarked on a trip from Damascus into the Hauran at a time when instability was the order of the day. The Syrian tribes, especially the Sardiya, who today live around Sabha and Subhiya and the north, were on the warpath. The Pasha of Damascus had already sent his cavalry and irregulars to meet them, and they succeeded in killing the Chief 'Arar and six of his companions, and taking thirty-one of his finest Arabian mares.

The Wahabys under Abdul Aziz ibn Saud had in the meantime advanced towards Damascus, but retreated when the two Ottoman governors of Damascus and Acre gathered their forces at el-Muzayrib. This general condition of unrest prevented Burckhardt from visiting Umm el-Jimal, but his geographical notes on the country south of er-Ramtha are outstanding. In all his diaries he writes about the inhabited villages, ruined villages, agricultural activity, population numbers, bedouins and their *khawa* (the tribute, sometimes referred to as *baksheesh*, that was exacted as protection money from

Fig. 3: John Lewis Burckhardt by H. Salt.

all travellers who required safe passage through the territories of the various tribes), administrative divisions – and many other topics.

Burckhardt's reports about Salt and life in it coincide with those of Seetzen, although they are much more elaborate. On his way to Kerak, he visited or wrote about every ruined village in the Balqa region. At that time, Amman's stream was full of small fish and on its southern side was a fine Roman theatre, the largest he had seen in the whole province of Syria.

In the summer of 1811, a battle was fought at Marj Ukke', near Na'ur, between the troops of the Pasha of Damascus and the Beni Sakhr, in which the former were routed. This resulted in a secret collaboration between the 'Adwan, the Pasha's troops, and the Ruwalla, to make a united attack upon the Beni Sakhr. Although the plot was well laid, the valour of the Beni Sakhr, who were assisted by a smaller faction of the 'Adwan and the Balqa tribes, proved a match for the united forces of their enemies. This battle was in reality a manifestation of the determination on the part of those settled in the Balqa to frustrate the attempts of the formidable Ruwalla to settle permanently in their lands. This strife continued for 100 years, and came to an end only in 1909 after another battle at el-Lubban, 12 kilometres south east of Amman. After this encounter, the Ruwalla moved northwards, and made their home in the areas east of the Hauran and Damascus.

Burckhardt also tells us that the inhabitants of Kerak, like those of Salt, were exempted, by their own strength in numbers, from all taxes and impositions[1].

Kerak had eight Madhafas (guesthouses controlled by the tribal sheikh) to Salt's four. This was so because every tribe had a Madhafa and there were more of these tribes at Kerak than at Salt. The three inhabited villages mentioned already by Seetzen were Kathurabah, el-'Iraq, and Khanzireh. All the other sites were ruined places. After three weeks in the city he accompanied Sheikh Yusif el-Majjali on his visit to Tafileh, a city of 600 houses. The whole district was governed by the El-Huwaytat whose sheikh had recently constructed a small castle there. From Kerak, Burckhardt continued southwards to Shobak, the principal town in the Sharah district, which had a population of nearly 100 families. Here again the Beni Sakhr were making their presence strongly felt.

On 22 August 1812, 74 days after he left Damascus on his trip to Transjordan, Burckhardt wrote:

> I was particularly desirous of visiting Wadi Musa of the antiquities of which I heard the country people speak in terms of great admiration, and from thence I had hoped to cross the desert in a straight line to Cairo. But my guide was afraid of the hazards of a journey through the desert and insisted upon my taking the road by Aqaba, the ancient Eziongaber at the extremity of the eastern branch of the Red Sea, where he said that we might join some caravans and continue en-route towards Egypt. I wished on the contrary to avoid Aqaba, as I knew that the Pasha of Egypt kept there a numerous garrison to watch the movements of the Wahabi and of his rival the Pasha of Damascus... I therefore pretended to have made a vow to slaughter a goat in honour of Haroun whose tomb I knew was situated at the extremity of the valley and by the stratagem I thought that I

should have the means of seeing the valley in my way to the tomb. To this my guide had nothing to oppose. The dread of drawing upon himself, by resistance, the wrath of Haroun completely silenced him (1822: 418-419).

The resourceful Burckhardt again got his way and was now set to discover Petra for the modern world. He was understandably anxious and worried, as his account reveals:

I was without protection in the midst of a desert where no traveller had ever been seen. Future travellers may visit the spot under the protection of ... an armed force; the inhabitants will become more accustomed to the researches of strangers; and the antiquities of Wadi Musa will then be found to rank amongst the most curious remains of ancient art. (1822: 421-422)

How very true indeed, for on 22 August 1812, Wadi Musa with its Siq, Kasr Faroun, (also known as the Khazneh, or Treasury), the Royal Tombs and Kasr Bint Faroun were seen for the first time in many centuries by a stranger who was also a good student of history. And yet he was not absolutely certain it was Petra as he wrote that same day in his journal: 'Whether or not I have discovered the remains of the Capital of Arabia Petraea I leave to the decision of the Greek scholars and shall only subjoin a few notes on these ruins' (1822: 431).

Fig. 4: James Silk Buckingham by W.T. Fry.

The third important pioneer traveller was James Silk Buckingham, an Englishman. He crossed from Nazareth to Salt on 23 February 1816, and his notes were published in 1825 in a volume entitled, *Travels among the Arab Tribes Inhabiting the Countries East of Syria and Palestine*. He explains the reasons for the delay and blames both Burckhardt and Mr William John Bankes as well as *The Quarterly Review*, a leading literary journal of the day, for having made unfounded charges of plagiarism against him, on the publication of his earlier work *Travels in Palestine* in 1821. It would appear that a degree of competition for a shared readership existed between these intrepid gentlemen, even in those chivalrous days.

Buckingham was an outstanding traveller of sound judgement, and a talented writer with an ability for accurate observation. In Salt, he, like Seetzen and Burckhardt, stayed at the house of the merchant and dignitary, Ayoub, and his notes about the town are in general similar to those of his two colleagues. He confirmed that there were thought to be 100 male Christians, most of whom came there to seek refuge from the persecutions of El-Jazzar (the Butcher), who was, until 1804, the Governor of Acre and Damascus, and famous for his fight against Napoleon. These Christians were chiefly from Nazareth, and today we can still count amongst them a few well known families. Buckingham was impressed by the Saltis' (the town's inhabitants) lack of fanaticism or bigotry, but complained that they were rather inclined to take it easy and spend time playing cards. From Damascus he continued to the Lebanon with the renowned Lady Hester Stanhope, before ending his journey in Aleppo. Unlike Burckhardt, Buckingham did not always hide the fact that he was an Englishman, during his stay at Salt, at least. However, during his travels, he wore Turkish dress enough to acquire the nick-name of 'Haj Abdullah' (Pilgrim Abdullah) (Buckingham 1825: 21-59).

We now come to the fourth adventure, that of Charles Leonard Irby and James Mangles, commanders in the Royal Navy. On 4 March 1818, after having worked for nearly 15 months unearthing the Temple at Abu Simbel, and then having spent three months in Palestine, they crossed the River Jordan, south of Tiberias. By this time they were a well-armed group of 11 people including Lord and Lady Belmore and Mr Legh Nevertheless, they needed protection, and for the while they made an arrangement with Ibn Fayiz, a young prince of the Beni Sakhr who was attended by his mace-bearer and ten tribesmen. They were all well mounted and armed, but Ibn Fayiz declined to take them to Jerash, because the Sirhan tribe, who were then at war with the Beni Sakhr, were encamped around it. They visited Salt and, unable to continue their travels in Transjordan, crossed the river instead for Jerusalem.

Determined to visit Petra and the Dead Sea, they joined up with Mr Legh and Mr Bankes and gave themselves Eastern names for the journey. Irby became Abdallah, and Mangles, Hassan. On 6 May 1818 they left Jerusalem, and assisted by guides of the Jahalin tribe, they travelled south and east. In the Ghor region south of the Dead Sea, they encountered a tribe of wild-looking people who wore leather aprons tied from the shoulders. Despite their alarming appearance, they were hospitable, and complained to Irby and Mangles of the treatment they received from the bedouin Arabs. After their sojourn with the tribes of the Dead Sea, the party continued to Kerak. Whilst there, they heard that the Wahabys had recently made an attempted assault on the town, and had encamped on the heights to the south. The inhabitants of Kerak boasted of having killed about 40 of their besiegers, firing on them with muskets from the arrow-sights of the castle. Soon after, they were able, through an arrangement negotiated by the Orthodox priest of the region with Sheikh Yusif el-Majjali, to ride south towards Wadi Musa and Petra. Sheikh Yusif accompanied them, but even so, the people of Wadi Musa stood in the way. For five days people gathered and messengers came and went, until at long last, on 24 May 1818, the party was permitted to enter Petra. They were the first pairs of European eyes to see the fabled ruins since Burckhardt had completed the feat a few years before (Irby and Mangles 1823: letters IV and V).

Last amongst this group of pioneers is the Frenchman, Léon de Laborde, son of Count Alexandre de Laborde, known for his literary works on Spain and Austria. Both father and son distinguished themselves as enterprising, diligent antiquarians and skilful artists. Léon, who visited Petra and Edom during February and March 1828, published his book, *Journey through Arabia Petraea*, in Paris in 1830. The trip started in Cairo, and after traversing the Sinai, he visited the Red Sea port town of Aqaba, with its Egyptian garrison. Letters from the Minister of the Interior to Muhammad Ali helped Laborde with the officials and with Abu Rashid, the sheikh of the Alawin tribe. The party then moved northwards through the Wadi Arabah and Wadi Ghurundal into Petra. He and his companions then enjoyed a relatively relaxed visit during which they visited all the important sites, beginning with the Khazneh, a name first coined for the monument by this group. They sketched, took measurements, copied inscriptions and drew maps during the eight days spent in the ruined city. Then they returned to Aqaba from whence they went to Ras Mohammad and then to the Monastery of St Catherine in Sinai. Laborde's contribution to the literature about Petra and Edom (also called Idumaea) is important as a worthy work on travel, but also as the first work to be published about the subject in the French language. The two previous works were in English, and it must have been a great joy for the learned Frenchmen of the day to have a book of their own.

These developments in the field of travel and discovery came to a standstill as the years of turmoil drew even closer. The Ottoman Empire was going through a period of stagnation and increasing instability, and Istanbul was trying to keep control over its governors in the Syrian provinces by inciting them to attack each other. Meanwhile, Muhammad Ali Pasha, the independent ruler of Egypt, was becoming stronger every day, and a number of the embattled governors were seeking his aid, or fleeing to Egypt when there

Fig. 5: Léon de Laborde.

was nobody else to receive them. As his ambition to possess Syria developed, so did his interference. He supported Abdullah Pasha, Governor of Saida, against Darwish, Pasha of Damascus, later giving asylum to Abdullah, as well as to Emir Bashir of Lebanon. However, in 1831, when Abdullah proved to be an ungrateful beneficiary of his years of protection, Muhammad Ali commanded his son, Ibrahim Pasha, to lead an expedition against him. In so doing, he conquered the Mediterranean port of Acre, and then, in four months, the whole of the province of Syria.

Nevertheless the instability continued in Transjordan, and insecurity was greatly increased by the Palestinian revolt against Egyptian rule in April 1834. When the leaders of the revolt took refuge in Kerak, Ibrahim Pasha followed them, and after a severe battle, the town was destroyed and its population forced to leave. Salt was also attacked and its castle demolished, while the Beni Sakhr at Zizia were dealt a heavy blow. No wonder then that travel in the region became somewhat unpopular until the Egyptian withdrawal at the end of 1840.

Despite all of the dangers and difficulties, the Englishman, A. W. Kinglake, became a rare traveller to visit the country in 1835, at the height of the disturbances. His book, entitled, *Eothen* (a Greek word meaning 'from the early dawn', or 'from the East'), was published a few years later. Considered by many as a great literary work, the book related his experiences and impressions whilst travelling in Turkey, Lebanon, Palestine, Transjordan and Egypt 'with the simplicity proper to his station' (Preface: x).

His foray into Transjordan was the result of a mistake by his Nazarene guide, who, on the road from Tiberias to Jerusalem, managed to take a wrong turn over the River Jordan. Although aware of the error, Kinglake kept quiet, thrilled with the prospect of an impromptu tour through the land of the wandering tribes. Thus started an adventure of two days and two nights which took the party all the way to the Dead Sea.

The reports of this traveller are most interesting as they give first hand information about the living conditions of a tribe in the Jordan Valley which was helpless after the Egyptian army had confiscated their arms, taken their camels and possessions, and shot their sheikh and every tenth man. Strangely, this terrible visitation of Ibrahim's troops worked in Kinglake's favour, as the unfortunate tribe now respected the Pasha – and by implication any of his acquaintances – to a degree which Kinglake found rather surprising:

> You would think that this conduct on the part of the Pasha might not procure for his 'friend' a very gracious reception amongst the people whom he had thus despoiled and decimated, but there is so much of vague, and undefined apprehension mixed up with his really well-founded alarms, that I can see no limit to the yielding, and bending of his mind when it is worked upon by the idea of power (Kinglake 1845: 203).

Kinglake's hosts were eager to assist him on his way. So the party could safely cross the River Jordan, they constructed a raft, and fastened to it several inflated animal hides which were usually used as water skins. Twelve of the men swam with the raft in its crossing. The animals were led into the water and forced to swim across the fast flowing waters of the Jordan.

In the same year, another traveller with different plans tried to visit the area by boat. Christopher Costigan, an Irishman, brought his boat by camels from Acre to Tiberias. But after three days on the Jordan, he abandoned the attempt and brought the boat, again on camel, to the north shore of the Dead Sea. For eight days during August he explored the Dead Sea in the searing midsummer heat – one of the most inhospitable environments on Earth. He fell sick with fever, and although he was transferred to the comparative cool and civilization of Jerusalem, the first man to attempt the navigation of the River Jordan died on 7 September 1835 from exhaustion[2].

In 1847, another attempt was made to explore the Dead Sea. Elliot Warburton visited the Jordan Valley, and published an account of his journey in his 1851 publication, *The Crescent and the Cross*. He was most struck by the natural beauty of the Dead Sea and the surrounding countryside, and was apparently surprised to find it so, given the morbid reputation of the place. He continued his account with a description of a delightful splash he and his companions were inclined to take in the buoyant waters of the Dead Sea, before remembering the dreadful cost the lake had exacted on previous travellers on its waters:

> Messrs Moore and Bek who attempted to explore the Dead Sea in 1837 found no bottom with 300 fathom of line; but their investigations were unfortunately soon interrupted, and Mr Costigan, the only other person who succeeded in launching a boat upon these waters, has left no trace of his discoveries (Part 2: 110).

Fig. 6: Dr Edward Robinson.

The English aristocrat Lord Lindsay embarked on an adventurous journey in the spring of 1837 that took him from Cairo to Damascus and Baalbek. His reports of the trip back to his mother in England were published in London in 1839. His journey to Transjordan started at the famous Convent of St Catherine in the Sinai. From there, he and his three English companions travelled across Sinai to Aqaba, and then on to Petra. His passage to Petra cost 4,500 piasters, the equivalent at the time of 45 gold pounds. He complained that maps were found to be of little use in this country and that his best course, therefore, was to ask the guides to go 'doghri', or straight to the appointed place.

From Petra the party travelled by way of the Wadi Arabah into Palestine, and from Nazareth back into Transjordan, to el-Husn, Umm Qais, Jerash, Amman, and Salt. He then continued to Damascus by way of the Hauran. He gave an excellent report about the hospitality of the people of el-Husn, particularly their guide, Sheikh Suleyman of the El-Husn, and confirmed that there was an Egyptian military presence in Irbid.

Edward Robinson is arguably one of the most significant figures in the history of Western scholarship of the ancient Levant. Although he travelled a well-trodden path in many cases, Robinson was a true pioneer in terms of the critical study of the region, as opposed to the adventuring and romantic impressions of previous travellers. An American pastor and professor of biblical literature, it was he who, together with his colleague the Reverend Eli Smith, made the first concerted study of biblical geography, analysing traditional identifications of biblical sites for the first time with a degree of healthy scientific scepticism. Although mostly associated with the country west of the Jordan, Robinson and Smith did make two trips to Transjordan. The first, in the spring of 1838, took them from the Sinai to Aqaba, where they made a study of the fortress and looked for any visible traces of ruins that might have been the remains of Ezion-Geber, King Solomon's Red Sea port of biblical fame. They had planned to carry on to Wadi Musa, but decided against going, due to the reported unreliability of the Alaween tribe, and their sheikh, Hussein (Robinson 1860a: 162-5). They were more successful on a second trip in May of the same year, starting from Hebron, and taking the route down to the Wadi Arabah and then into the Wadi Musa, on to Kerak, Tafileh, and Ma'an, before arriving at Petra. They returned by way of the Dead Sea to Jerusalem in early June. Robinson and Smith made numerous studies of the environment and monuments of Edom, the Wadi Arabah, and the Dead Sea, marking a new chapter in the scientific study of the region. In particular, Robinson, by a masterful study of ancient sources and the recent observations of fellow travelers, was able to identify positively the site of Petra as being the famous city of antiquity (1860b: 103-195).

In 1839, the renowned and much reproduced painter, David Roberts, visited Transjordan. However, Roberts, with his great interest in Egypt and Nubia, limited himself as far as Transjordanian sites to Petra and Aqaba alone. His lithographs have left an indelible image of the ancient sites of the Near East on Western imagination, and in no instance is this truer than of Petra (see Roberts 1843).

In the same year as Robert's visit, two years after Lindsay reported on an Egyptian presence in northern Transjordan, the Egyptian Pasha withdrew his armies from the province of Syria. Almost immediately, the Ottomans tried to apply the 'Hatt-i-Serif of Gulhane', also known as the 'Reforms of the Tanzimat'. This Imperial Rescript of the Rose Chamber was promulgated by Sultan Abdulmejid on 3 November 1839. The decree was issued with a sincere desire to preserve the Empire, and improve the conditions of its inhabitants. Its timing was calculated to gain the support of the European powers against the rebellious Pasha of Egypt, and naturally, this new attitude brought about hopes for a more relaxed atmosphere, and had the effect of enticing a larger number of travellers to the region.

Sir Henry Layard was another adventurous English traveller who, in 1839, became so bored with life in London that he decided to ride on horseback across the Ottoman Empire and Persia to reach Ceylon. In the spring of 1840 he was eager to explore the area of Petra, Moab, Jerash and the east of the Dead Sea, and while trusting that an Englishman could succeed better than others, he also believed firmly in his own capacity to overcome whatever difficulties lay ahead. Three Jahalin tribesmen from around the Dead Sea joined him on the strength of letters from the Egyptian Pasha of Jerusalem, but despite these measures, they were attacked in Petra by the Budul tribe. On his way to Kerak, Layard was again attacked and robbed, and his life was saved only when he managed to seize the sheikh of the attacking party and hold him hostage. In Kerak he met Sheikh Suleiman ibn Fayiz of the Beni Sakhr, 'A tall handsome man of dignified appearance', who, after some differences, became a charming host, entertaining Layard 'very hospitably as his guest' (Waterfield 1963: 37). In the encampments at Kerak, he had first-hand contact with their way of life. The sheikh showed him his suit of chain armour, which had been handed down from one generation to the next, perhaps from the time of the crusades, and was still worn in battle. Layard visited Amman and Jerash, but had difficulties in reaching Damascus when he found out that the plague had broken out in the area. Once in Aleppo he prepared for his long journey to Mosul and Baghdad. When he arrived in Mesopotamia, the ancient man-made mounds and the stone monuments in the great city of Nineveh fired his imagination and he became the most celebrated scholar of Mesopotamian antiquities. Later, Sir Henry Layard, or 'Layard of Ninevah' as he became known, served as British Ambassador to the Ottoman Empire between 1877-1884, and retired from a political career towards the end of the century.

Conditions in Transjordan were always changing, and the well-laid plans of travellers were often thwarted by the unpredictable behaviour of some of the bedouin tribes. A few years after the visit of Lord Lindsay in 1837, a fellow countryman was unable to accomplish a similar visit. In 1842, the Reverend George Fisk travelled from Cairo through the Sinai to Aqaba. Although he held lengthy negotiations with Sheikh Hussein, chief of the 'Alaween tribe and Lindsay's companion, who monopolized the route through Petra to Hebron, it was not possible to strike a deal. Fisk had to relinquish hope of visiting Petra and contented himself with visiting Palestine and the Jordan Valley (Fisk 1842: 188-190).

Gregory M. Wortabet of Beirut (written by him as Bayroot), visited Transjordan in 1843. His book, *Syria and the Syrians*, was published in London in 1856. Evidently, conditions in the Balqa region were not good for travel, as he limited himself to an apparently almost compulsory excursion to the Jordan and the Dead Sea;

> it is considered a necessary appendix to a pilgrimage to Jerusalem and few are the travellers who visit the last mentioned place without making the said tour. The tour is generally performed in three days, and the traveller will find that he will require a tent for his night in Jericho as there are no houses in it (223-224).

Another important traveller of this period was the Finn, August Wallin, known as Abdul Wali, who travelled in the region of the northern Hijaz. His trip started in April 1845 from Cairo to Aqaba with the purpose of going from there across the Sharah to el-Jauf, just to the south-east of Wadi es-Sirhan. He gives a good report about the tribes in Sinai, the Tiaha, Tarabin and Huwaytat and the people of Ma'an, which was the major market town for the pilgrimage caravan whilst on its way to and from Mecca. The large tribe of Esh-Shararat

Fig.7: Dean Arthur Stanley of Westminster, etched by Charles Laurie.

is mentioned by him in detail since it was the main tribe in the area between Ma'an and el-Jauf (Wallin 1979: 150).

In 1847, 12 years after the tragic attempt made by Christopher Costigan on the descent of the River Jordan by boat, another expedition was made, this time by a naval officer, Lieutenant Molyneaux of *HMS Spartan*. The voyage, narrated in a paper given to the Royal Geographical Society on 28 March

1848, tells how he transported the ship's dinghy from Beirut to Tiberias by camels, and from there, departing on 23 August, proceeded with five men, two of whom were English. For a great part of the time, he was on the bank, and frequently out of sight of the boat which had four men to pull her and one to steer. On the 30th, they were attacked by fifty Arabs who fired shots at the party and captured the boat only to return it to the explorers at Jericho. In early September, Molyneux and his party spent several days on the waters of the Dead Sea, before returning with the boat in tow to Jerusalem. However, this adventure ended, like Costigan's, in tragedy. Molyneux, who prophesied in Jerusalem that he would become sick, was seized by fever on arriving in Beirut, and died on 3 October 1847 (see Molyneaux 1848: 104-180 for an account of the expedition).

Next in the succession of explorers came W.F. Lynch of the U.S. Navy, the first American to travel extensively in the area since Edward Robinson a decade earlier. His mission was to travel in boats down the River Jordan and then to navigate the Dead Sea. His book, *Narrative of the United States Expedition to the River Jordan and the Dead Sea*, was published in Philadelphia in 1850. His notes contain a good deal of information about tribal warfare in the area, particularly concerning a battle in April 1848 between Aqila Agha, the Mughrabi Chief (who was an important ruler for some 40 years in northern Palestine) and the Beni Sakhr on one side, and the Adwan on the other. Aqila accompanied Lynch and his party from the Dead Sea into Kerak, and in order to secure the good behaviour of people in the area he brought with him the young prince of the Beni Sakhr, 'a powerful tribe of whom even these fierce Arabs stood in Awe' (360-361).

During his stay in the town, Lynch was struck by the misfortune of the people of Kerak, who, that May, had suffered a seventh consecutive year of locust swarms decimating their crops. Despite the presence of the prince of the Beni Sakhr, the travellers still had difficulties in Kerak, but managed to return to the Dead Sea with the entourage of the Christian sheikh of Kerak, and thence by way of the convent of Mar Saba to Jerusalem. Aqila, in order, to avoid another encounter with the Adwan, decided to take a different route on his own journey back to western Palestine. He and his party took sufficient flour and water for five or six days, struck into the desert to Zizia on the Haj Road, and from there back west to the vicinity of Lake Tiberias (346-396).

In the winter of 1852-3, a distinguished English cleric, Dean Arthur Stanley of Westminster, made a journey that took him and his three companions from Egypt to the Lebanon. His journeys to Transjordan would take him by way of the Sinai to the Wadi Arabah and Petra. Like many of his contemporaries and predecessors, as might be expected, Stanley was particularly concerned with the study of the country in relation to biblical scholarship, and his observations on the landscape are always in reference to the biblical accounts of the wanderings of the Israelites before entering the 'Promised Land' of Canaan. In this respect he was very much in the same mould as Edward Robinson before him. His remarks on the dangers of travel in the region of Petra reveal an adventurous, less scholarly, man: 'Fifty years hence, when our friend Sheykh Mohammad has put down the surrounding tribes, Petra will have lost half its interest; but now the failures and dangers are sufficiently recent to form part of the first impressions of the place' (Stanley 1856: 86). Stanley was more fortunate than many of his predecessors in reaching Aaron's Tomb on Mount Hor, before continuing with an exploration of the city of Petra itself. Ever concerned with the biblical texts, Stanley proposed that Petra was the true identification of Kadesh-Barnea, the oasis where, according to biblical tradition, the Israelites had encamped for forty years.[3]

Syria and Palestine was a Victorian bestseller, and remained in print well into the twentieth century.

Dean Stanley was particularly struck by the absence of reliable maps for the Levant throughout his journey. As a biblical scholar, he saw this as a serious impediment to future study in the region. His solution was to propose the establishment of a learned society devoted to the accurate mapping and description of the Holy Land for the purposes of scholarship. Together with his friend, Sir George Grove, Dean Stanley finally achieved this ambition, with the founding, in London in 1865, of the Palestine Exploration Fund.[4]

The renowned French Orientalist, Melchior de Vogue (1829-1916), made a trip east of the Jordan and into Syria in 1864. He was a fine architectural scholar, and recorded the remains of many sites in his ground breaking study, *Le Temple de Jerusalem*, published in Paris in the same year. This volume was primarily an architectural study of the Temple Mount in Jerusalem, with plans and drawings of the existing monuments (such as the Dome of the Rock and the el-Aqsa Mosque), as well as in-depth discussions as to the possible appearance of the previous monuments on the site, at that time identified as the Jewish Temples of Solomon and Herod.[5]

For this purpose, de Vogue made a study of many of the ruins of sites in other parts of the country, including in particular, those at 'Iraq el-Emir'.

Hot on the heels of de Vogue, another Frenchman, Felicien de Saulcy, a member of the French Institute, was accompanied by a few of his countrymen when he visited Transjordan in 1850 and 1851. He strongly believed that it would be of no advantage to science if his party were to tread again the beaten paths already traced by hundreds of other tourists, and if they did not visit areas still unexplored. They therefore went to Ghor es-Safi and made contact and arrangements with the El-Jahalin, El-Huwaytat, and the Beni Sakhr. The sheikh of the Beni Sakhr asked de Saulcy about Napoleon Bonaparte and upon learning that France was a Republic, remarked; 'A country without a Sultan is like a horse without a rider or a tribe without a Sheikh' (de Saulcy 1854: 301). In Kerak, the party met with many difficulties, and as he could not make the necessary arrangements, de Saulcy missed the trip to Petra, returning instead to Jerusalem by way of Hebron and Bethlehem. The English copy of his comprehensive reports and ride notes were published in book form in London in 1854 with the title *Narrative of a Journey round the Dead Sea and in the Bible Lands*.

1851 was the year when the Governor of Damascus, already well established in the Hauran, decided the time had come to control the area of Jebel Ajlun to the south in Transjordan. The region was organised into an administrative district, or 'Qada', and a governor was appointed to run the new unit (Rogan 1999: 24). This was followed during the next two decades by a period of systematic subjugation of the tribes in the Balqa. Salt became another Qada in 1867 immediately after the 'Adwan were defeated in a battle to the south of Wadi es-Sir.

Just after this encounter, the role of the Palestine Exploration Fund (also known as the PEF, or 'Fund') becomes more apparent. The new society's first venture into Transjordan took place in 1867 when the area was visited and surveyed on its behalf by Lieutenant Charles Warren of the Royal Engineers, and a party of other officers and NCOs from the regiment, whose reports were published in the *Palestine Exploration Fund Quarterly Statement* (1870: 284-311, 381-388). Warren reported that on leaving Jerash they found all the surrounding villages deserted and empty at their approach, perhaps in part due to their military appearance, despite their peaceful intentions.

Using three-dimensional surveying techniques for the first time in the region, the Royal Engineers accurately surveyed 400 square miles between Salt and Jerash and 250 square miles in the Jordan Valley, taking a large number of photographs of the sites and landscapes they encountered. Photography had been developing at a quick pace since 1859, and was an ideal (although at this time extremely cumbersome) tool for accurately recording the physical appearance of ancient sites and monuments as they then were. The photographer, Corporal Henry Phillips R.E., stands out as one of the true pioneers of scientific photography in the region.

Fig. 8: The PEF Survey Team of 1867-70, Mediterranean Hotel, Jerusalem. From left, seated, Charles Warren, the Reverend Mr Barclay and Corporal Henry Phillips, the photographer. Standing behind is Jerius, the party's dragoman, and reclining in front is Mr Eaton. Henry Phillips, August 1867.

Fig. 9: The 'Rob Roy' at the mouth of the River Jordan, at Lake Huleh. Watercolour sketch from his field note book by J. MacGregor, 1869.

Fig. 10: The Ordnance Survey of Sinai Expedition Members, 1868-9. From the left: the guides, Hassan and Salem, Prof. Edward H. Palmer, Lieut. Henry Palmer, R.E., Captain Charles Wilson, R.E., Reverend F. W. Holland, and C. Wyatt, Esq.

Another attempt to navigate the River Jordan was undertaken in 1869 by J. MacGregor, whose best-selling book entitled, *The Rob Roy on the Jordan*, was published in London the same year. During this trip the author also cruised in the waters of Egypt, Palestine and Damascus and described well the way of life in these lands. MacGregor's canoe trip down the Jordan took him from the river's source at Banias, through Lake Huleh into the Jordan Valley north of Lake Tiberias, and ending at the exit of the River Jordan from the south end of the lake. From this point he took leave of the River Jordan, and explored instead the Kishon River of western Palestine. He presented his sketchbook from the journey to the PEF in 1880, where it has remained ever since.

In the years 1868 to 1869 an expedition was mounted by the Ordnance Survey in collaboration with the PEF. This was the Sinai Survey Expedition headed by Captain Charles Wilson and Lieutenant Henry Palmer of the Royal

Engineers. Another expedition member, lending it academic credibility, was Edward H. Palmer, Professor of Arabic and Fellow of St. John's College, Cambridge. The PEF decided, in 1869, to extend the survey into the Negev and Moab. This expedition was led by Professor Palmer, with Charles Tyrwhitt Drake as naturalist. Palmer's book of the mission, *The Desert of the Exodus*, was published by Harper & Brothers of New York in 1872. It gives detailed reports about the southern part of Transjordan including the Arabah, Petra, and Moab as far as Mount Nebo at the northern end of the Dead Sea.

During the late 1860s and early 1870s, however, travellers were not encouraged to venture into the countryside on account of the state of instability and tribal warfare. A good example of this was the sacking of er-Ramtha in 1869 by the joint forces of the Beni Sakhr and El-Adwan. It was, therefore, some years before exploration resumed in earnest. When it did, one of the first scholars was H.B. Tristram, Canon of Durham, who visited in February 1872 and published his work, *The Land of Moab*, in London in 1873. In the same year Henry C. Fish became the first American to tour the Balqa. His notes were published in Haverford County, Connecticut, in 1876).

Fig. 11: H. B. Tristram, Canon of Durham.

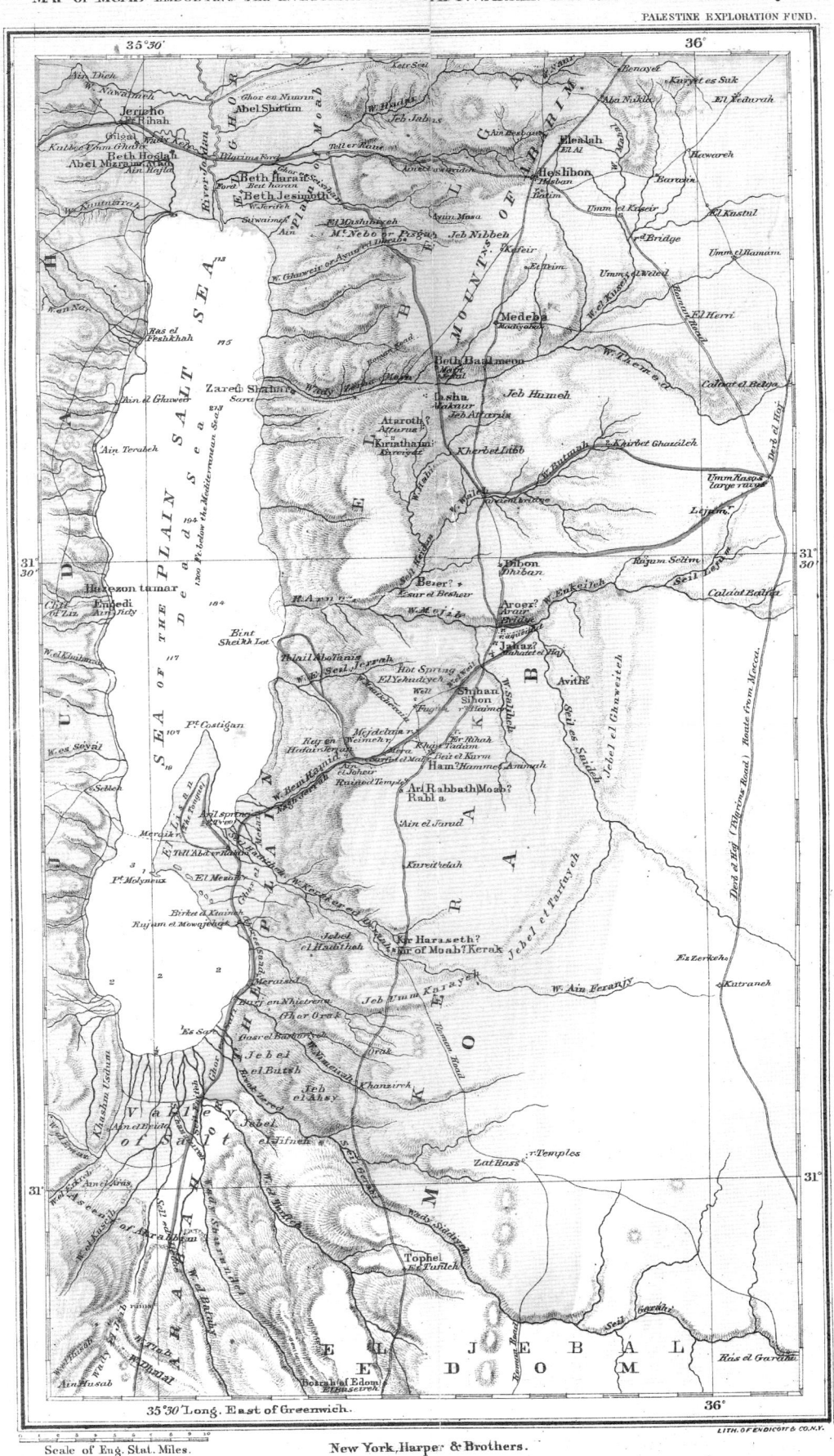

Fig. 12: 'Map of Moab Embodying the investigations of Capt. Warren R.E. and E.H. Palmer Esq. Palestine Exploration Fund', New York 1872. (Courtesy of R.S. Abujaber.)

American interest in Transjordan increased significantly in 1870, with the establishment of the ill-fated American Palestine Exploration Society (APES), which undertook to conduct a geographical and archaeological survey of the country east of the River Jordan. The ultimate aim of this was to join the results of the American survey with those of a similar operation the PEF were conducting in western Palestine, to form a large map of the whole of the southern Levant. In 1872 the APES acquired the services of Lieutenant Edgar Z. Steever of the U.S. Army for this purpose, accompanied by the Reverend Professor John Paine of New York, who was employed as Archaeologist and Naturalist. In 1875, Steever and Paine were replaced by Colonel James C. Lane and Dr Selah Merrill, who were joined later by the photographer Tancrede R. Dumas. The survey continued until August 1877. The results of the survey were handed over to the PEF in 1878, which was when the shortcomings of the American mission were first properly understood by the PEF Committee. Ultimately, it was found to be impossible to publish the two maps together because of the considerable inaccuracies apparent in the American work.

The APES was finally disbanded in mid-1880, only seven years after its establishment, leaving behind only a handful of copies of a 13-sheet printed map of the Eastern Survey, together with a volume of accompanying notes by Selah Merrill, and a volume of statements and reports of the society.[6] Merrill published an additional book, *East of the Jordan*, in New York in 1881.

Fig. 13: Camp of the American survey party at Salt, by T. R. Dumas, 1875. In the centre of the picture, a man holds the huge standard of the local sheikh, seated to his right (possibly Gublan of the 'Adwan tribe. (Courtesy of Harvard College Library, Boston.)

The Reverend William M. Thompson had been Chairman of the Beirut-based 'Steering Committee' for the APES expedition. His bestselling *The Land and the Book* was first published in London in 1878. Thompson had been a missionary in Syria for some 30 years, and had a great deal of first hand knowledge of the region. *The Land and the Book* was a popular work, designed for the general public rather than for the professional student. Years later he published a second volume, *Lebanon, Damascus and Beyond Jordan*, in which the author's name is followed by the words 'Forty five years missionary in Syria and Palestine'. He visited many places in Transjordan and his book contains numerous photographs, illustrations and maps of the area (Thompson 1886).

The next visitor to Transjordan was the famous Englishman, Charles M. Doughty, who joined the Syrian pilgrimage caravan in the Hauran on 13

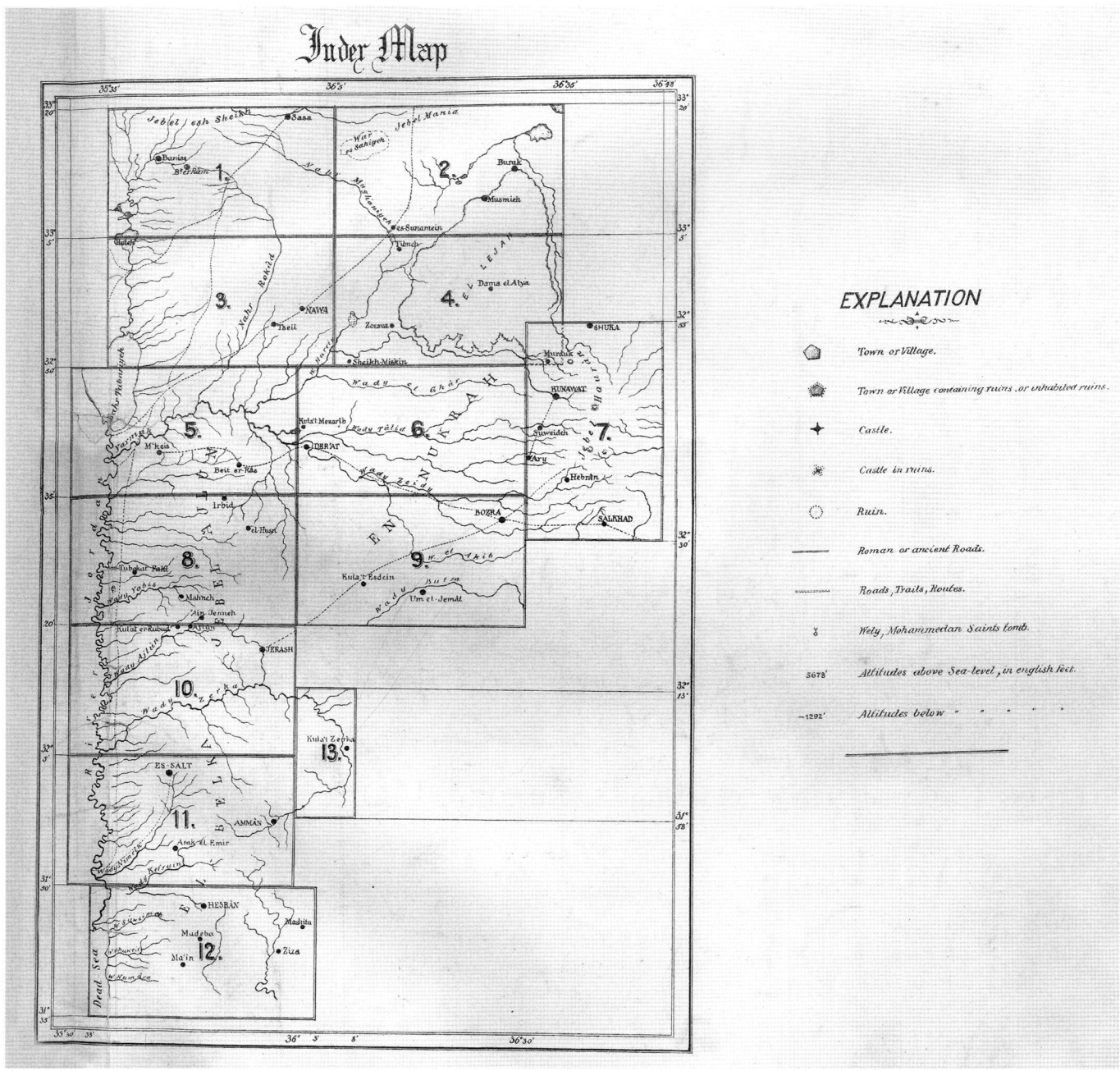

Fig. 14: Key Map from the APES 13 sheet map of Survey East of the Jordan, drawn by R. Meyer. Photo-zincographed by the Ordnance Survey in Southampton, 1879.

November 1876. Posing as a *hakim* (doctor), and not hiding the fact that he was a *nasrani* (a Christian), 'Khalil Effendi' as he was known, travelled all the way to the Hijaz. On the way he stopped in at all of the Transjordanian Hajj stations and managed to visit Petra. His famous literary work, *Travels in Arabia Deserta*, was originally published in 1888. The 1921 edition has an introduction by his friend, T.E. Lawrence.

In 1879, a South African born Englishman and missionary by the name of Lawrence Oliphant crossed the river and spent few months studying the possibilities for a Jewish settlement in Transjordan. His book, *The Land of Gilead*, was published in London in 1880, and is a record of travels undertaken in pursuance of this idea which occurred to him shortly after the conclusion of the Treaty of Berlin in 1878[7].

Having visited Turkey on three former occasions in the years 1855, 1860 and 1862, Oliphant felt a great urge to improve the prospects of Palestine. His favoured means of achieving this was a plan for 'Jewish Emigration from the countries in which they are now persecuted to the land upon which their longing eyes are fixed as their future home in Palestine' (532). One scheme,

Below left. *Fig. 15: Lieutenant A.M. Mantell R.E. O. Schoefft.*

Below right. *Fig. 16: Lieutenant Claude R. Conder R.E. at Elisha's Spring, Jericho. H.H. Kitchener, 1874-75.*

Fig. 17: Members of the Arabah Survey expedition relaxing in their tent. From the left: Dr Edward Hull, Mr H.C. Hart, MA, Dr Gordon Hull, the photographer, and Major H.H. Kitchener. E.G. Hull, 1883-4.

published in the *Jewish Chronicle* in September 1880 was to arrange for the travel of 100 families of Romanian Jews to Palestine. Another was to bring Jewish settlers to the Balqa region of Transjordan, in the hope that their enterprise and industry would be of benefit to the area, and would bring stability to Ottoman rule (504-6).

The next PEF expedition to Transjordan commenced in 1881. The 'Survey of Eastern Palestine' was led by Captain Claude Reignier Conder of the Royal Engineers (who had led the Survey of Western Palestine some years before), with Lieutenant Mantell R.E., as photographer. Within three months, and with the assistance and protection of Sheikh Gublan of the Adwan tribe, 510 square miles were triangulated and 610 site names were obtained. During the survey, in March 1882, Conder was charged with accompanying the British princes Albert Victor and George, Prince of Wales, on their tour of Palestine. This 'Princes' Tour', was the first time Christian royalty had visited Transjordan for over 600 years. Sheikh Fallah of the Adwan tribe accompanied the tour during their sojourn in Transjordan, which lasted from 10-15 April, and during which they visited 'Iraq el-Emir, Amman, Salt, and Jerash (Conder 1882 and 1889: 282-3). After crossing back into western Palestine, Sheikh Fallah presented the Prince of Wales with a memento of his trip to Jordan, a crucifix with a figure of Jesus Christ, which had reputedly been found at Hesban.[8]

Unfortunately, and despite the obvious prestige of the Royal Tour, official permits from the Ottoman government to continue the expedition were refused, and the Survey of Eastern Palestine was finally abandoned in late 1882. Together with Warren's work a few years before, this survey formed the core of the volume on Transjordan in the PEF's famous thirteen-volume reference work, the *Survey of Western Palestine* (Conder 1889)[9].

Two years later, in 1883, The Palestine Exploration Fund undertook the Wadi Arabah Survey (which was part of a geological survey of the whole of the southern Levant, including the Sinai Peninsula). The survey was conducted

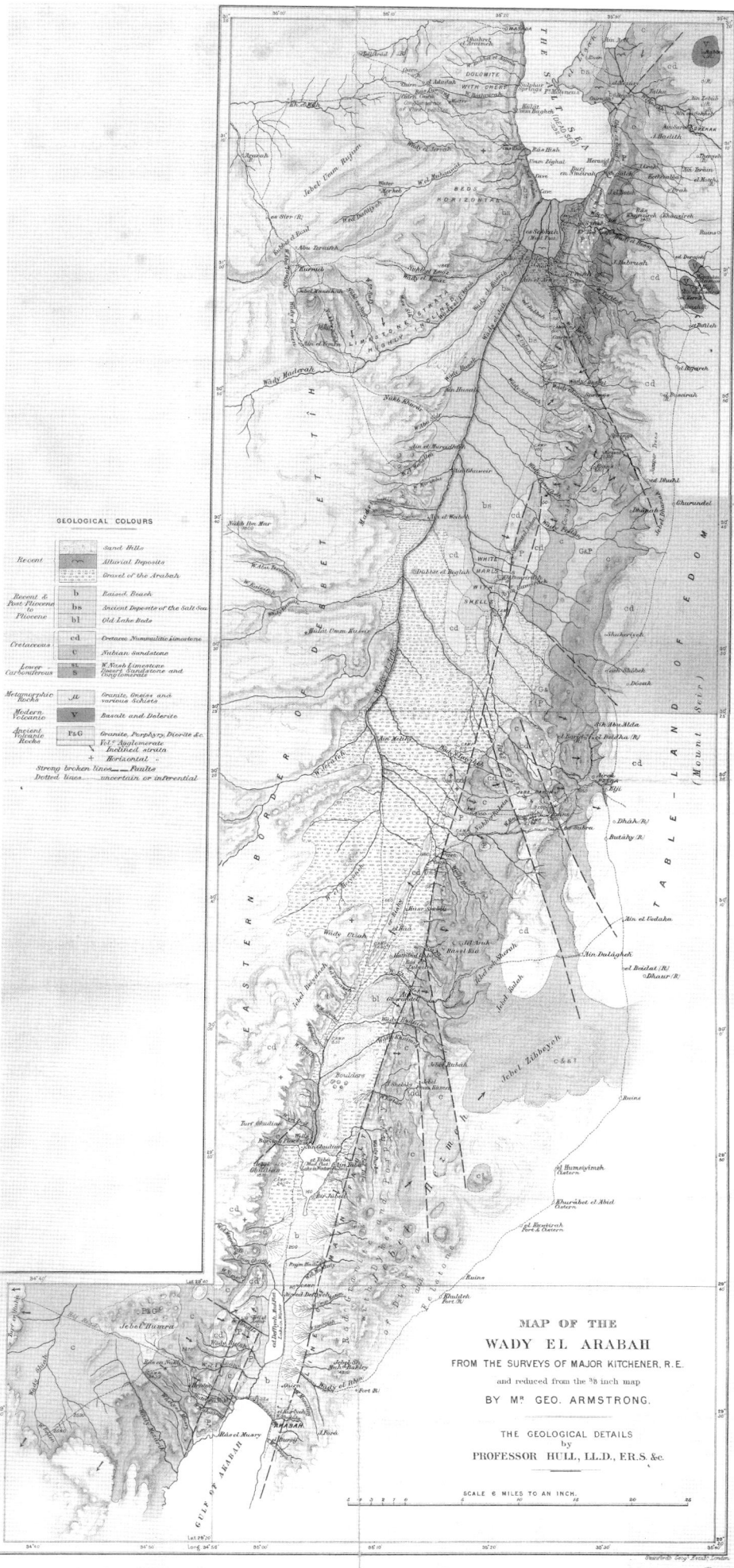

Fig. 18: 'Map of the Wady El Arabah from the Surveys of Major Kitchener, R.E., (1883-4) and reduced from the 3/8 inch map by Mr Geo. Armstrong. The Geological Details by Professor Hull, LL.D., F.R.S. &c.'

under the leadership of the geologist Dr Edward Hull, with a young Lieutenant H. H. Kitchener conducting the geographical survey. Dr Gordon Hull (the son of Edward) was the expedition's photographer (Hull 1886).

The year 1891 witnessed the second visit of the renowned American geographer, George Adam Smith, to the area: his first in 1880 had been limited to western Palestine alone. He could not help remarking that between the two dates great changes had affected many of the most important historical and sacred landscapes – due in part to the activities of European colonists, and by the escalating rivalry between the Greek and Latin Churches over building projects. His seminal reference work on the historical geography of Palestine and Transjordan, *The Historical Geography of the Holy Land*, referred to the works of many of the writers and travellers mentioned in this chapter. He was convinced that 'the real exploration achieved during the last twenty years has been the work of no one nation, and its effectiveness is due to its thoroughly International character.' (1906: xi).

Gottlieb Schumacher, a German national, was an architect and railway engineer employed on the Haifa to Damascus Railway project. He was profoundly interested in the ancient history of the region, and took the opportunity that his employment afforded him to conduct a survey of the ancient monuments of the region through which the railway line was to be built. Lawrence Oliphant, his neighbour at the Haifa Temple Colony, put him in touch with the PEF in London, as a potential English language publisher of his survey of this northern part of Transjordan, which had already been published by the German Palestine Exploration Society, the 'Deutscher Verein zur Erfroschung Palestinas'. As well as his survey results and map being included in a later edition of the *Survey of Western Palestine* in 1897, a number of his books were published by the PEF. Three of his books of relevance here are, *Across the Jordan*, *The Jaulan*, and *Abila, Pella and Northern Ajlun* (Schumacher 1886, 1888 and 1889 respectively).

In spite of the increasing number of visits made by travellers to Transjordan in the late nineteenth century, few of them were made to the Kerak area, which had been out of Government control for many years, and remained so until 1894. Among those who did venture there, and who experienced considerable difficulties, were Sir Gray Hill and his wife. Their visit took place in 1890, the book of which, entitled *With the Beduins*, was published in London in 1891. In Hill's account, the 'Keraki' as he refers to the people of the area, did not come across in the best of terms, exacting ever greater payments of money from unfortunate travellers, and subjecting two English missionaries, Mr and Mrs Lethaby to 'continual insults, threats, and robberies' (206). The Hills themselves were held prisoner in the camp of Sheikh Khalil with the demand of a payment of 60 napoleons, which they did not have. They were deprived of food and warmth, and Lady Hill became increasingly ill: 'We must try something. We cannot go on like this much longer. In the previous night the cook has been beaten, the food at the fire snatched away in spite of him, and half our bag of bread stolen. The Keraki threaten to starve us into payment. They will sell us nothing. Our charcoal is failing' (219). The unfortunate

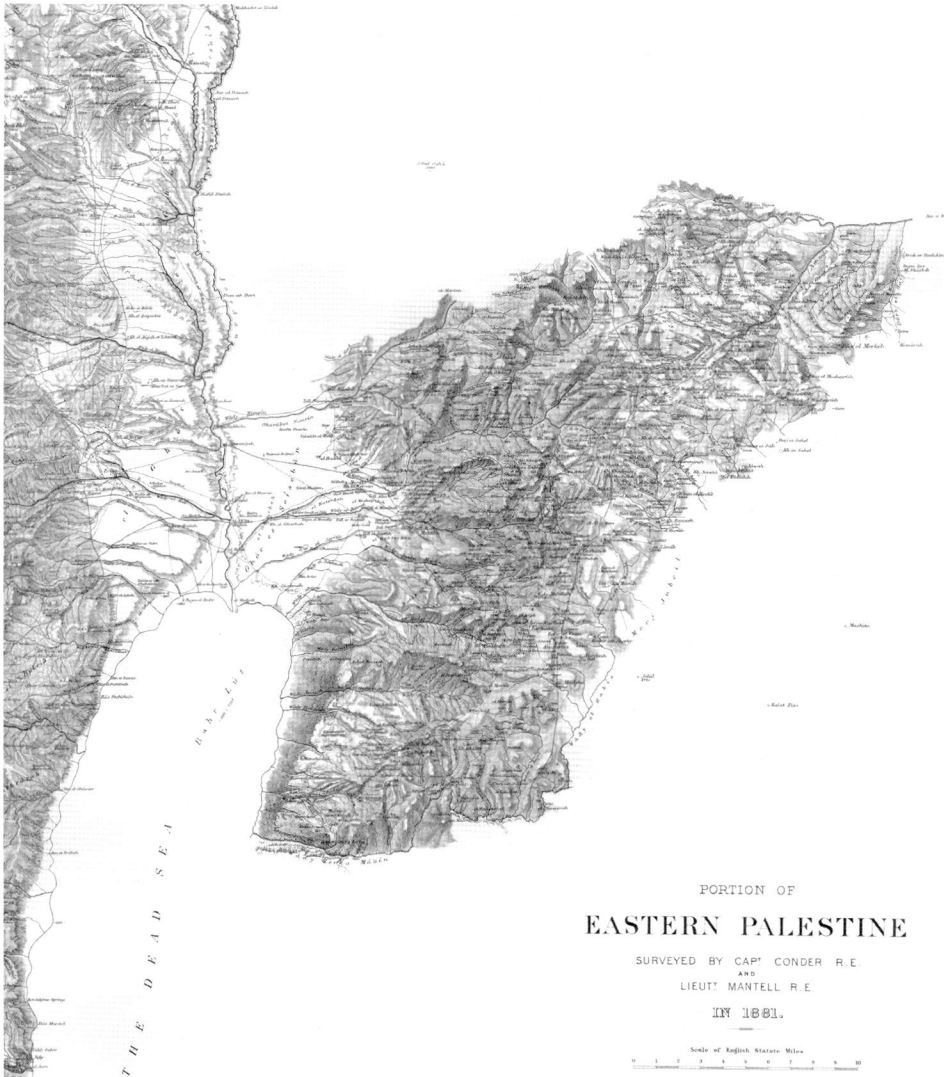

Fig. 19: Map of the Survey of Eastern Palestine conducted by Captain Claude Conder R.E. and Lieutenant Mantell R.E. in 1881.

travellers had no option but to send a messenger with a letter to the Consul in Jerusalem requesting the money for their release. They waited a full five days until their messenger returned with the ransom, and they were released from captivity (221-30). It could have been that their enforced detention in Kerak, and the reporting of the incident in the European press, induced the British envoys and consuls to lodge strong protests in Jerusalem, Damascus and Istanbul. This might have also been one of the causes for the dispatch of an expedition of around 2,400 troops to Kerak in 1894 under General Hussain Hilmi Pasha. This operation saw the start of law and order in the south, and an end to Kerak's freedom from the payment of taxes and government control. This new stability had an immediate positive impact on the volume of travel and exploration in the area.

In 1895, taking advantage of the new stability, two separate expeditions investigated the archaeology and ethnography of Transjordan. Both of these were published in the PEF's journal, the *Quarterly Statement* in 1895, and in 1898. The first was made by Frederick Jones Bliss, a seasoned excavator west of the Jordan, and son of the founder of the American University of Beirut. With the cooperation of the Turkish authorities, and in the new

Fig. 20: 'The Dead Sea Observation, the Rock at Ain Feshkah, Mr Hornstein holding the tape.' F.G. Newton, 1911.

climate of law and order, Bliss made an official visit on behalf of the PEF to the regions of Gilead and Moab in the spring of 1895, primarily with the intention of surveying, recording, and photographing the ancient monuments, and of updating the work of previous surveys in the light of new discoveries. Of particular interest were new discoveries, somewhat off the beaten track of the time, including the monuments of Qasr Bshir, and Mushatta (Bliss 1895).

The second visit, by Charles Alexander Hornstein, was less 'official' in nature, but was nevertheless an important expedition. Hornstein, a resident of Jerusalem, and subscriber to the Fund, visited an area similar to that surveyed by Bliss, but his explorations took him further south and east, to Ma'an, and Petra. His description of Ma'an is idyllic: 'The inhabitants are very polite and seem altogether of a class superior even to the Fellahin around Jerusalem. There are a great many gardens and orchards, with streams of water flowing through them' (Hornstein 1898). Today, Ma'an is a functional and rather ordinary place built out of the ubiquitous concrete of the late twentieth century, and covered with the dust of the desert and oil from the tanker-trucks that pass through on their way from Aqaba to Amman.

Both the Bliss and Hornstein trips were particularly valuable because of the number of quality photographs that they took, and the range of subject matter that interested them. Hornstein, in particular, was as much interested in the people of Transjordan as he was in the monuments and landscapes, and this is apparent in his photographs.

Just before the turn of the century, Antonin Jaussen, a Catholic priest, who was evidently also connected to the French Intelligence Department, made his researches in southern Palestine and Moab. He spent a few years in the area and studied the conditions prevailing in Madaba after it was resettled in 1880 by the three Christian tribes who moved into it from Kerak. He recorded his findings in an interesting book, *Coutumes des Arabes au Pays de Moab*, published in 1907.

Another turn of the century traveller was Alois Musil, who was probably connected with the Imperial Court in Vienna. He lived for many years amongst the Ruwala tribe, and befriended their sheikh, Nouri esh-Sha'alan. His experience in the Jordanian countryside was recorded in an extensive three-volume work entitled, *Arabia Petraea* (1907).

It was at this time also that a team of two German researchers, Rudolf Brunnow and Alfred von Domaszewski, visited Transjordan (1897 and 1898). They toured the country, starting from Amman and Madaba, and then to Aqaba by way of Petra. Their focus was the Roman period remains of sites like Jerash, Amman, and the ruins in the Hauran of north Transjordan and southern Syria. In 1904, their account was published in a large three-volume work, *Die Provincia Arabia*.

Soon after, a group of American scholars embarked on a survey expedition to the archaeolgical remains of central Syria, which also included many sites in Transjordan. Many of the sites had been visited by de Vogue back in the early 1860s, and the plan was to update his work and make a careful photographic record of the monuments. The expedition, known as the American

Archaeological Expedition to Syria (AAES), was led by a young Princeton scholar, Howard Crosby Butler. From October 1899 to June the following year, the expedition examined numerous sites, from Antioch in the north to Petra in the south. Although the results of the survey were published, the photographs were subsequently mislaid, but even without these, the survey represents a great step forward for the study of the ancient past of the area MacAdam 1986: 241-244).

Following the success of the American Expedition, Princeton directly sponsored another survey of the area which took place, again under the directorship of Butler, in the years 1904-5, and once more in 1909. These were the seminal 'Princeton University Archaeological Expeditions to Syria'. The survey made exhaustive studies of the classical period sites in the region, including 'Iraq el-Emir, Amman (Philadelphia), and Umm el-Jimal. The final publication runs into four volumes, all published between 1907 and 1930.

In 1902, two more American academics, William Libby, Professor of Geography at Princeton, and Franklin Hoskins of the Syria Mission in Beirut, made a journey that took them from Beirut, down the Jordan Valley, to Petra in the south. Their most valuable contribution to scholarship was the rediscovery of the second 'High Place' of Petra, behind el-Habis, which they describe in detail in the second volume of their book of the journey, *The Jordan Valley and Petra*, which was published in London in 1905 (191-207).

The last of our travellers to Transjordan were the archaeologist Duncan Mackenzie, (best known as Sir Arthur Evans' assistant at the Knossos excavations in Crete) and the architect Francis Newton, who were, at the time, employed by the PEF to excavate in Western Palestine. During their employment, both men were keen to visit Transjordan, and so in 1910 they embarked on a trip that would include a survey of the dolmens and ruins of Ammon and Moab, and the city of Petra.

Mackenzie had excavated and studied all over the Mediterranean world, and like Conder before him, was intrigued by megalithic remains found at many sites throughout the whole region, from the Greek Argolid to Sardinia. Although some of Mackenzie's theories are now out of date, his careful study of the dolmens and towers was a serious attempt to get to grips with the pre-classical archaeology of Transjordan. The photographs and reports from this trip remain an important source of factual information and observations concerning many sites and monuments that have long since disappeared with the advance of modern civilization (Mackenzie 1911a and 1911b).

In Petra, Mackenzie and Newton teamed up with Professor Gustav

Fig. 21: Frederick Jones Bliss.

Fig. 22: 'Ain Shems, the excavators.' The picture shows Duncan Mackenzie on the left and Francis G. Newton on the right, in 1912.

Dalman, the director of the German Protestant Institute of Archaeology in Jerusalem, on a remarkable study of the architectural decoration of the Khazneh, about which more shall be said in due course (Dalman 1911).

Safety and security in any venture to the east were still very much a concern, but by 1910, things seem to have improved somewhat. In his reports back to the PEF in London, Mackenzie described their experiences of travel in Transjordan in glowing terms, the local tribes being hospitable and friendly towards them (1911a).

Things were very quick to change, however, and an editorial note accompanying Mackenzie's report describes subsequent massacres in the area through which the travellers had passed in total safety just a few weeks before. Transjordan, it would seem, was still a region of extremes and unpredictability for inhabitants and foreigners alike, and this over 100 years after Seetzen made his journey to this strange and adventurous land.

The numerous explorers mentioned here came for different reasons, sometimes as independent travellers, and sometimes as members of larger expeditions, but all were ambitious and adventurous individuals. With few exceptions, they all went back and reported what they had seen in their own way, leaving us with a legacy of travel writing, and the major source for information about this unknown part of the world until the imposition of firm Ottoman rule in 1851. Lady Gertrude Bell, who was amongst the first to visit at the start of the twentieth century, probably expressed the thoughts of all travellers, when quoting her attendant Mikhail, she wrote: 'And please God Inshaha'allah, you shall journey in peace and return in peace to your own land' (1919: 340).

NOTES

1   Burckhardt mentions 550 families in Kerak, and 480 in Salt.

2   This unfortunate attempt is described on pages 22-25 of the book published in London 1939 by the Society for promoting Christian knowledge. The author, Rev. R.J. Whiting of the American Colony of Jerusalem was well known for his articles in the *National Geographic Magazine* and his article about the trip was published on pages 781-808.

3   Stanley 1856: 92-98. This particular theory has long since been disregarded.

4   For an account on the founding of the PEF, its objectives and principles, see Besant 1895: 125.

5   Substantial remains of Herod's first century BC temple precinct have been identified, but as yet, no remains of an earlier temple have been found.

6   PEF Archives: PEF/DA/APES. An article on the subject of the APES expedition to Eastern Palestine by F. Cobbing will be published in the January-June 2005 edition of the *PEQ* (Vol. 137.1)

7   The Treaty of Berlin was concluded on 13 July 1878 after a whole month's conference held in Berlin under the chairmanship of Prince Bismark and with the participation of Lord Beaconsfield (Disraeli), Lord Salisbury and other representatives of European Powers and Turkey.

8   This relic is made of black iron and was acquired by R.S. Abujaber from a dealer in Wales in 1988.

9   The various PEF surveys conducted in the nineteenth century were all published as part of the PEF's monumental work, the Survey of Western Palestine. During the 1880s and 1890s, 13 volumes were published as follows: 26 sheets of 1 inch map of the country south of Tyre and north of Beersheba, up to the Jordan River. (C.R. Conder & H.H. Kitchener). Accompanied by: 3 volumes of Memoirs written by C.R. Conder and H.H. Kitchener; 1 Arabic and English Name List. (C.R. Conder, H.H. Kitchener, and E.H. Palmer); 1 Volume of Excavations in Jerusalem by C. Warren and C.R. Conder; 2 map boxes of plans of Jerusalem drawn by C. Warren and his team; 1 volume of Flora & Fauna (Canon H. B. Tristram); 1 Volume of Special Papers (C. Wilson, C. Warren, C.R. Conder, H.H.Kitchener, E.H. Palmer, *et al*); 1 Volume of General Index (H.C. Stewardson); 1 Volume of Geology (The Survey of the Wady Arabah)(E. Hull); 1 Volume of the Survey of Eastern Palestine (C.R. Conder & A.M. Mantell); Charles Warren's survey of the country around Jerash and Amman, and Conder & Mantell's map of Eastern Palestine were added to reprints of the 'Great Map', as it was known, as was Gottleib Schumacher's own survey of the north of the country around Ajlun, Irbid, and the Sea of Galilee.

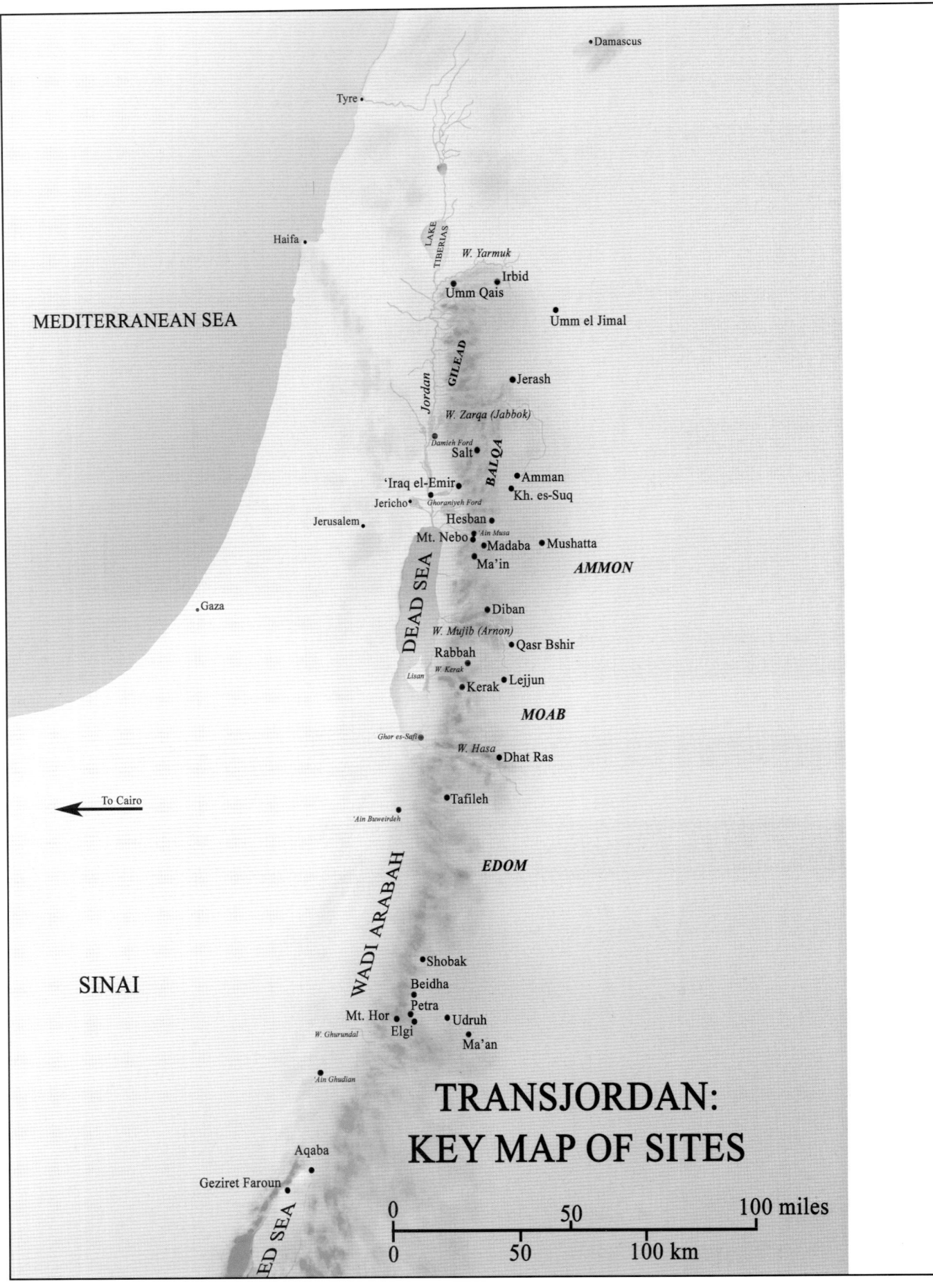

Chapter Two

The People and the Land

Fig. 23: Key map of photographed sites in Transjordan (F. Cobbing, 2004).

The geography of Transjordan, as well as its administrative divisions over the ages, has been the subject of many studies. However, for our purposes, we shall focus on the conditions that prevailed during the second half of the nineteenth century when photography developed into an established profession.

From the Iron Age through to late antiquity, Transjordan consisted of kingdoms and territories based on natural geographical boundaries, many of which still form the administrative boundaries today; the kingdoms of Edom, Moab, and Ammon, and the regions of Gilead and Bashan, for example.

The modern state of Jordan consists of these regions, as well as further territories previously part of the Kingdom of the Hijaz far out to the East, including Aqaba and Ma'an, which were given to Jordan in 1925 (Al-Madhi and Musa 1959: 248-9). An additional part of the coastline at Aqaba was added in 1965 when the boundaries of Jordan and Saudi Arabia were redrawn (Musa 1996: 311).

A population census in 1922, in the early days of the Transjordanian Emirate, and before the new territories just mentioned were added, estimated the number of inhabitants to be around 225,400 of whom approximately 122,400 were settled, and the remaining 103,000 nomadic (Al-Madhi and Musa 1959: 311).

As mentioned before, today's population is closer to 5.6 million, putting a huge strain on the country's resources, especially water. This huge increase is in part due to the political upheavals of recent years in the Middle East. The relative stability of the modern Hashemite Kingdom has often made it the most viable option for resettlement for many dispossessed people from other parts of the region.

Two hundred years ago, things were very different. The accounts of the early travellers to Transjordan mentioned in the previous chapter reveal a sparsely populated country, especially in the more arid regions to the south and east. Seetzen, writing in 1806, tells how he had to take a sufficient quantity of bread from Salt for his trip to Kerak because the area in which he was travelling had no settled population (1810: 37). Burckhardt, throughout his book, *Travels in Syria and the Holy Land*, often gives descriptions of the populations in the few inhabited sites he visited. When comparing these accounts with those of the 1922 estimates, the total population in 1812, at the time of Burckhardt's visit, cannot have amounted to more than 90,000 people including bedouins. Many villages and old cities were in ruins, and Jerash, Philadelphia (the modern capital Amman) and Madaba were completely uninhabited.

Burckhardt is particularly informative about the land and its inhabitants at this time, especially regarding the tribute paid by the settled populations to the nomadic tribes, and the frequent instances of inter-tribal conflict and warring. During his stay at Souf, a few kilometres to the north of Jerash, he discovered that every household produced its own supply of gunpowder. It was manufactured by grinding, in a large stone mortar, a combination of one part sulphur, five and a half parts saltpetre and one part of the poplar wood readily available from the densely wooded hills around Ajlun. This supply, together with the abundance of quality pasture land to the south in the Balqa was, Burckhardt thought, ample explanation for the never-ending territorial disputes between the tribes of the area, particularly the Ruwala of 'Aneze (1822: 250).

Seetzen and Burckhardt happened to visit Transjordan before the occupation of Syria by the forces of Muhammad 'Ali, Pasha of Egypt. In 1831, the Egyptian army, under the able leadership of Ibrahim Pasha, Muhammed 'Ali's son, occupied Syria. Eventually, after some ten years, and as a result of a campaign waged against him by the Ottoman, British, French, and Austrian governments and local Arab irregular forces raised from different areas in the province, he was forced to evacuate the territory. During these ten years, because of the lack of security in Transjordan (despite the attempts of Ibrahim Pasha to spread stability and security in the land), travel was very limited.

The distribution and livelihoods of the population in the different areas of the country were basically related to the nature of the land. Whether the people living in it were dependent more on agriculture than animal husbandry was determined by environmental conditions and natural resources. In the populous north, in the Ajlun area, most people were farmers, and the villages, especially those in the hilly country, had enough manpower to resist the occasional bedouin exactions that threatened them from time to time. The eastern part of the area, however, which was open to the *badiya* steppe desert, and stretching from er-Ramtha to Mafraq, suffered from bedouin raids until as late as the 1930s. Some villages in the area were settled by bedouin tribes such as the Sardieh, Beni Sakhr, Beni Khalid, El-Issa and the Sirhan. Completely settled now, these eastern areas still claim their tribal allegiances, especially when there are elections for Municipal Councils or Parliament. To the west there are the areas of what used to be called during the nineteenth Century 'El-Mashaikhat', or 'The Chiefdoms'.

The main settlements of this northern area, between the Yarmuk and Zarqa Rivers, in Ottoman times include Beit Ras, Irbid, el-Husn, Ajlun, Souf, and Mafraq. Among the ancient sites are Umm el-Jimal, and five of the cities of the Decapolis; namely Gadara (Umm Qais), Capitolias (Beit Ras), Arbila (Irbid or Qwailbeh), Pella (Tabaqat Fahl), and Gerasa (Jerash).

With such riches of the ancient past to be explored, this area was particularly attractive to Western travellers intrepid enough to venture from the relative safety of Western Palestine or Egypt.

Moving south, the nineteenth century traveller would come to two regions; the Balqa to the west, and the Zarqa Governorate to the east. In his famous study, George Adam Smith wrote that ancient Peraea 'was probably identical with the modern Balqa, or the region between Jabbok and Arnon. In one passage, Josephus says that it stretched from Pella, or just south of the Jabbok, to Machaerus, or just north of the Arnon, and from Jordan to Philadelphia (1906: 53). Smith translated the Greek word 'Peraea' as simply meaning 'the land across.' The main city, Salt, was practically an independent city state, governed by its own people, under the umbrella of the Adwan tribe. In 1867 the Ottoman administration sent an expeditionary force to the area to bring it back under its direct control. After defeating the joint forces of the Adwan and Beni Sakhr, it entered the city and installed a governor and a permanent garrison.

The operation exacted a devastating toll on the rebels, who lost 50 men on the battlefield, with many others being wounded. The Ottoman forces, in marked contrast, sustained no fatalities, and minimal injuries[1].

The stability and security brought by the establishment of direct Ottoman rule made all the difference to the prosperity of the area.

This was observed by Laurence Oliphant, who, in 1880, wrote:

> The inhabitants find that the security which has resulted therefore attracted strangers with capital and that the Saltis have materially benefited by this sacrifice of their liberties. Salt has become by degrees the mercantile entrepôt for the whole region east of the Jordan. The merchants trade with the Arabs [meaning bedouins] and advance them money on their flocks and crops. The latter are thus imperceptibly acquiring commercial instincts, for nothing civilizes a man so rapidly as teaching him to borrow money and run into debt. (201)

Oliphant estimated that the population of Salt numbered around 6,000, double what it was in Burckhardt's time 70 years earlier (200). He stayed for some time in Salt, making observations about the daily life of its inhabitants. His comments on the system of land ownership are revealing. Apparently, no deeds or titles to land were in existence, and ownership, or claims to ownership, were based entirely on prescriptive right alone. Small wonder then that disputes were common.

Agriculture in the area was primarily based on viticulture. The grapes, he remarks, are of a high quality, adding rather ruefully that 'excellent wine could be made, if the art was properly understood' (206). Oliphant goes on to state that the area under cultivation by the inhabitants of Salt was 1200 feddans, a feddan being the area that could be ploughed by one yoke of oxen in a day (ibid: 203).

Even this early on, attempts to cultivate the less obviously fertile lands further to the east were being attempted. Oliphant was an enthusiastic supporter of colonization in the area, and these agricultural experiments were of great interest to him. One large experimental wheat farm of 60 feddans at el-Yaduda particularly attracted his attention. He names the owner of this farm as Abou Jabr (Salih Abujaber, the great-grandfather R.S.Abujaber), and describes him as a protestant Syrian (in reality he was an orthodox Christian), and the only man outside of Salt who lived in a house in the whole of the Balqa area: 'That he should have been able to build himself a house and live in it unmolested in the heart of the Beni Sakhr Arabs and distant a day's journey from Salt is an evidence of the rapid strides which this country is making towards order and good government'. (270-271)

As well as having a large settled population in centers like Salt, the Balqa was the territory of the two largest Jordanian tribal federations, the Adwan and the Beni Sakhr. Travellers mentioned them often, and many a trip had to be cancelled as they were unable to acquire safe-conduct in the different districts. The Adwan were semi-settled bedouins who were chiefs of the tribal federation that included all the settled and semi-settled people in the Balqa. They spent winter in the cultivated lands and pastures of the Jordan Valley, and moved upwards into the plateau west and north of Amman in summer. Their paramount chiefs during the nineteenth century were the Salih clan headed by Sheikh Dhiab and his son, Ali el-Dhiab. However, they had to contend all the time with their cousins the Nimr clan headed, during the same period, by Sheikh Gublan and his family. Gublan was famous amongst travellers, and was usually the chief who arranged the protection they needed during movement through the countryside.

It was as a local guide and protector that Sheikh Gublan and the Adwan tribe accompanied Claude Conder and his party on the Survey of Eastern Palestine. Conder was struck by many aspects of the nomadic life, and the close relationship the sheikh had with his people. On one occasion, at a ford of the River Jordan, a poor Arab and his wife and daughter were attempting to cross the river. The two women were afraid, as the waters of the Jordan are very rapid, and can be treacherous, and so the man 'invoked the help of Gublan with that peculiar mixture of affectionate respect and simple familiarity which is one charm of nomadic society' (1885: 321-322). Without further ado, the women were given rides across the river on the horses of two of Gublan's men, who then returned to the eastern shore.

Gublan was, Conder notes, 'most exasperatingly greedy for money', but, as he readily admits, the payment received by the sheikh from the travellers was shared out most generously amongst his people. But this generosity was not without an ulterior motive, as Conder goes on to explain: '... it is by such lordly munificence and hospitality that a great Sheikh retains his influence among poorer and weaker tribes in time of peace' (ibid: 322).

The other important tribal federation in the Balqa, the Beni Sakhr, was also engaged in travel activities. In 1839 Layard of Nineveh was perhaps the first Western traveller to be entertained by this tribe. The wealthy and powerful Sheikh Suleiman Abu Jneib el-Fayez gave 1000 piasters (£10) and a beautiful robe of Damascus silk to Sheikh Ahmad el-Majjali as payment for Layard's safe passage and escort. After a while, Sheikh Suleiman stopped arguing about money and became a charming host, entertaining Layard as his guest. During this trip Layard rediscovered the famous Palace of Mushatta with its intricate stone carvings (Waterfield 1963: 37).

A more extensive encounter with the Beni Sakhr occurred in 1873, when Canon H.B. Tristram, supported by a grant of £100 from the British Association in Edinburgh, visited Transjordan. Arrangements were made with Fendy el-Fayez, the sheikh of the Beni Sakhr, for his son, Sattam, to escort the party through the north of Moab. However, Sattam was delayed by the Adwan tribe, who claimed exclusive rights to convey travellers north of Hesban, and threatened extreme violence on Sattam if these rights were infringed. In the event, all was bluster it would seem, as Sheikh Gublan was actually negotiating the marriage of his daughter to Sattam, and this alliance had been forged out of personal admiration for the young man rather than for any political advantages that might have been gained (Tristram 1873: 4-5).

The area starting a few kilometers south of Madaba, which was only resettled in modern times in 1880, marked the start of the tribal domain of the Beni Hamida. They became famous amongst travellers and archaeologists after

BEYOND THE RIVER

Fig. 24: 'Sketch of a basaltic stone with Moabite Inscription discovered by me among the ruins of Daban [ancient Dibon]. On the 19th of August 1868.'
Pen & ink drawing by Father A. Klein.

the discovery by Father A. Klein on 19 August 1868 of the Mesha Stela in Diban, also known as the Moabite Stone. This inscribed basalt stela commemorates the battles of Mesha, the King of Moab, against the Israelite Omride dynasty in the ninth century BC, and details building programmes in the capital (Diban). It was the first instance of a character from the Old Testament (King Mesha) being confirmed as an historical person by mention in a source other than the biblical texts themselves. The inscription itself was in a Semitic language very closely related to contemporary Hebrew and Phoenician, and was named 'Moabitic script'. As well as the stone's

significance for biblical history, the inscription remains one of the earliest extensive examples we have of the alphabetic script that we still use today.[2]

Western interest in the Mesha Stela was considerable, as one would expect, and this aroused the curiosity of some of the Beni Hamida tribesmen as to its monetary value. Searching for hidden treasure, they split open the stone, expecting to find valuables inside. Of course they did not, and so the most significant inscription from the region's ancient history was broken into fragments. The ownership and information of the stone was much contested by the various Western nations obsessed by its recovery. Charges and counter-charges of secrecy and transparency were levelled at the great and good, particularly Captain Warren of the PEF, the Frenchman Charles Clermont-Ganneau, and the stone's German discoverer, Father Klein. The fragments of the stone were eventually reassembled, and it is now on display in the Louvre.

The interest created amongst scholars by the Mesha Stela overflowed into the bizarre story of what has become commonly known as the 'Shapira Affair'. In Jerusalem, in 1872, a collection of strange artifacts was put on sale by Moses Wilhelm Shapira, a well-known dealer in antiquities to western collectors and museums. Shapira claimed that these ceramic and stone figurines and vessels came from Diban, and were of the same vintage as the Mesha Stela (in other words, from the ninth century BC). They were often decorated with script characters that seemed very similar to those of the stela, and this convinced Claude Conder of the PEF, among others, that the artifacts were genuine. However, on closer analysis, the inscriptions were shown to be nonsensical, and the artifacts themselves were shown to be of recent manufacture, hailing from a workshop in Jerusalem rather than from Diban. A French diplomat and archaeologist, Charles Clermont-Ganneau, who was also in the employ of the PEF, was the principal agent in uncovering the deception. The affair had the academic world in a spin for a number of years, and resulted in the ruining of Shapira's reputation as a reliable source of antiquities. Whether he was directly implicated in the forgery, or was the victim of an elaborate hoax is still a matter of debate, but he was never able to regain his business. He committed suicide in Rotterdam in 1884.

The Shapira Affair is the first well-documented instance of antiquities forgery in the Levant, a regrettable practice that continues to be an issue of concern for archaeologists and scholars to this day.[3]

The 1870s witnessed a certain feeling of stability and security in comparison to previous decades. People seemed to be more certain of their safety, and travellers started to refer to the bedouin escorts they had as guides or companions instead of guards or armed men. This was a direct consequence of the increased attention afforded to the countryside by the Turkish authorities after having installed an administration in Salt in 1867. Earlier, in 1851, the same exercise had been applied in the Jebel Ajlun area north of the Zarqa River. Conditions in the Kerak area and southwards had to wait until 1894 when Hussein Hilmi Pasha entered the town at the head of an expeditionary force of a few thousand, establishing a return to direct administrative control in both Kerak and Ma'an (Peake 1934: 177).

Writing in 1876, Selah Merrill, archaeologist with the American Palestine Exploration Society (APES), described in some detail the composition of the population in Transjordan at the time. He mentions 70 Greek Orthodox Christian families, living at el-Husn, and describes schools at el-Husn, in addition to those at Kerak, and Salt (1881: 353). The semi-settled, semi-nomadic population consisted of the Adwan tribe, with 400 tents, the Beni Abbad, with 600 tents, and the Beni Hasan with 1,000 tents. The Beni Hamida, together with

Fig. 25: '*Mr Shapira's collection of Moabite idols. Part of the second German contingent.*' *H.H. Kitchener, 1874.*

other tribes in the Moab region, was estimated to consist of 3,000 or more tents. The 'Aneza, a completely nomadic tribe, numbered somewhere between 2,500 and 3,000 tents. Merrill does not mention the settled tribes of the Balqa, who are estimated to have had about 1,000 tents, or the famous Beni Sakhr, who numbered about 1,500, (ibid: 471).[4]

At this time, the settled population of the Sharah region, including Tafileh and Shobak, could have been about 5,000 souls. As for the town of Ma'an, G. A. Wallin, who visited the area in 1845, mentioned that it had 200 families, in addition to 20 families in Ma'an esh-Shamieh nearby: 'They are, in general, a healthy and strong built people of the most prominent Syrian type, able to raise a force of 150 or as others told me, of 300 well armed young and gallant men. Trusting in this force, the inhabitants, in our times, have begun to make head against the claims of the nomads, which a great many sheikhs of the neighboring tribes of Shararat, Huwaytat and Aneze exact of them' (1979: 122).

The large confederation of tribes in the south was led by the Huwaytat tribe, who, together with their allies, numbered as many as 3,000 tents. They claimed south Jordan as well as parts of the northern Hijaz and the Sinai. They exacted the *khawa*, bedouin protection money, from the settled population and from the weaker tribes in the area. They, like the tribes of the northern part of Transjordan, did not allow free passage to travellers in their domain, who were often compelled to pay this unofficial tax.

In 1839, in an incident referred to briefly in Chapter 1 (p.25), Henry Layard, and his companions Antonio and Awad, were attacked just outside Kerak by the Aranat, a notorious clan of robbers. Layard (a man of considerable courage, and the proud owner of a suitable firearm) grabbed hold of the sheikh of the clan and threatened him with death if any of his party were harmed. Evidently, the sheikh was convinced by Layard's persuasive arguments, and the party continued unmolested (Waterfield 1963: 37).

With some of the journeys to the Levant, and all of those of an early date, the travellers themselves had to make many of their own arrangements. They had to arrange their passage on boats, and their accommodation or camping arrangements. They had to purchase their own provisions and equipment, and, last but not least, conclude deals with those who accompanied or protected them. Commercial travel agents were unknown throughout much of the nineteenth century, until the establishment of Thomas Cook's Tours in 1841. From the very beginning of the PEF's explorations in the 1860s, Thomas Cook was extremely involved in the successful operation and organization of many of the expeditions to both sides of the river Jordan. The firm, now named Thomas Cook & Son, acted as the PEF's banker out in the field, issuing traveller's cheques against the PEF's bank account, initially from their Cairo office, and subsequently from Jerusalem. In addition, they assisted with the hiring of local dragomens and other personnel essential for any expedition. Frequent reports on the PEF's operations in the field appeared in Cook's *Traveller's Gazette*. The relationship was so close that, upon the death in 1899 of John Mason Cook, Thomas Cook's son, the PEF wrote an official letter of sympathy to his widow in recognition of his services to exploration, and recorded his passing in the *Quarterly Statement*.[5]

Cook's involvement with the PEF would eventually lead to the development of a vigorous tourist trade in the Levant as a whole. For, in assisting the PEF's explorers on a practical level, he was in the perfect position to take advantage of the increased knowledge of the region afforded by their new maps and descriptions. Initially, Cook ran commercial tourist trips within the UK alone, but soon expanded to ventures in Europe and Egypt. In 1869, tours were offered to Palestine, and within a few years following the surveys of the APES (1875-1878) and the PEF (1881-1882), extensions across the Jordan were being advertised. However, these attempts were premature, largely due to the lawlessness of the country, and regular tours were only properly available by 1890. These tours included trips to the area east of the Dead Sea, passing through Machaerus and Madaba, and visiting Hesban. Arrangements for visits to Petra began to appear in Cook's *Traveller's Gazette*, Thomas Cook's own monthly travel magazine, from 1907 onwards. Transjordanian destinations started to appear regularly in Cook's literature around 1908, and from that date, the Palestine brochures included various itineraries covering Petra, Madaba, Amman and Jerash in particular. A single brochure for 'Petra and the Land beyond Jordan' dated 1930, covered a seven-day tour from Jerusalem to Amman, Petra, and Jerash, including the services of a private dragoman. The package was offered for £27, a reasonable price considering that 40 years earlier, a similar trip could have cost as much as £200.[6] Thomas Cook & Son continued actively to develop tourism in the region, establishing the first hotel east of the River Jordan in Amman in 1922. The Philadelphia Hotel was situated near to the ancient citadel, and here at last, travellers could rest in safety and comfort in the fast developing capital of the new Hashemite Principality.

By the beginning of the early twentieth century, the stability of the region had improved to such a degree that travellers' safety no longer had to be guaranteed by the payment of *baksheesh* or *khawa* to the local tribal sheikh. This unpopular tax was replaced by the pleasanter custom of giving presents for recognition of courtesies or favours, as is the custom today.

By the end of the nineteenth century, the country east of the River Jordan had changed dramatically. An important development was the settlement of the land in the Balqa region, and the conversion of the land from open pastures to wheat-growing farms. El-Yaduda was already a prosperous large estate in 1860, thanks to the pioneering spirit of its owners the Abujaber clan. Madaba became another important estate in 1880 when three clans of Christians in Kerak settled there. In the following years the Khairs settled at er-Rajeeb, and the Bisharats at Umm el-Kundum. A clan of the Abujabers settled at el-Juwaideh, the Masarwah clan at Sahab and the Nabulsis settled at Hesban. From 1879 onwards, Circassian and Chechen tribesmen settled in villages like Na'ur, Wadi es-Sir, Amman, Swayleh, Zarqa and es-Sukhen. The bedouin clans of the Beni Sakhr settled all the ruined villages south of el-Yaduda up to the boundary with the domain of the Beni Hamida.[7] By the year 1900 there was no unclaimed land left in the whole area. Living conditions at the same time had improved greatly, and many a traveller was persuaded to take a trip that was considered a great adventure only 30 years earlier.

Transjordan, as Albert Hourani wrote in 1988, had been for many centuries a place where the changing relations between nomadic pastoralists and sedentary cultivators have formed one of the main themes in its history, a feature that is true of many areas of the Levant. The natural resources of Transjordan can often be used for either purpose, and the balance between the settled agriculturalists, who use the limited water supply for their crops, and the nomadic pastoralists, who require the water and grazing lands for their flocks, is shifting and precarious. It is a constant ebb and flow between the 'desert and the sown' which is a defining characteristic of the country. Presently however, the shift is firmly in favour of a settled agrarian and urban society, and the nomad has been banished to the edges of the desert. As Haurani observes, 'In the lands lying east of the Jordan, the expansion of agriculture has taken place in little more than a century. That of a government in a still shorter space of time.' (Abujaber 1989: xii).

NOTES

1 Enclosure 2 in Dispatch no. 63 from Damascus to Constantinople dated September 10, 1867 as appearing in the records of the Foreign Office in London.

2 See *Palestine Exploration Fund Quarterly Statement* 1870: 169-183, 281-283; 1872: 117: 1874: 2, 126 and 1876: 181-182 for the reporting of the discovery of the Mesha Stela and subsequent discussions on its significance. For a modern translation of the text, see Gibson 1971: 71-83.

3. The affair of the Moabite Pottery, as told by those involved, can be read in the journal *Athenaeum* for the period relevant, and in the *Palestine Exploration Fund Quarterly Statement* 1872-1878. See also Silberman 1982: 131-146 and associated references.

4 The bedouin tent is comparable to a household or family unit, consisting of about 5 individuals.

5 PEF Minutes for the meeting held on 7 March 1899, and *Palestine Exploration Fund Quarterly Statement* 1899: 269.

6 In 1872, Canon H. B. Tristram was provided with a grant of £200 by the British Association to conduct a geographical survey of Moab (see Tristram 1873: 3).

7 For more information about the different stages of this settlement operation, *see* Abujaber 1989.

LEUR TENTE.

Chapter Three

The Rift Valley: Barrier and Gateway

Detail of a bedouin sheikh and his horse in the Jordan Valley. (See Fig. 44.)

BEYOND THE RIVER

Separating Transjordan from the western regions of the Levant is the Rift valley. This deep geological fissure in the earth's crust, the northernmost extension of the Great African Rift, was the gateway – or barrier – to all travellers from the west to the lands of adventure that lay beyond. Writing in 1896, the geographer George Adam Smith described this feature as: 'a rift more than one hundred and sixty miles long (from just below Lake Huleh, where the dip below sea-level begins, to the point on the Arabah south of the Dead Sea where the valley rises again to sea level) and from two to fifteen broad, which falls from the sea-level to as deep as 1,292 feet below it at the coast of the Dead Sea. In this trench there are the Jordan, a river nearly one hundred miles long, two great lakes respectively twelve and fifty three miles in length'. (1906: 469)

In the northern reaches of the rift, by Lake Galilee and beyond, the climate is pleasant, with abundant fresh water and vegetation. However, as the descent below sea level begins, culminating at a depth of 417 metres by the shores of the Dead Sea,[1] the climate becomes ever warmer, resulting in stifling temperatures in the Jordan Valley, Dead Sea and Wadi Arabah in the summer months. As a result, human habitation on the more southerly areas has tended to be more sporadic and temporary, although the abundance of fresh water in the Jordan Valley has encouraged settlement since ancient times, in spite of the almost unbearable summer heat. The region as a whole receives some rain in winter, particularly in the Jordan Valley, which increases the fertility of the region. Approaching from the direction of Egypt and the Sinai, the traveller would first encounter the southern end of the rift, the Wadi Arabah, a series of interconnected basins, 180 kilometres long, running from the northern end of the Gulf of Aqaba to the southern end of the Dead Sea, with an average width of only ten kilometres.

Fig. 26: The 1883-4 PEF survey party resting in their tent at the end of a hard day in the field, taken by Gordon Hull. From left to right: George Armstrong, Professor E Hull, Henry Hart, Major H.H. Kitchener, and Reginald Laurence. Photograph by G. Hull, 1883.

This was precisely the route taken by the PEF's survey party in the winter of 1883-84. Their task was to conduct a geological survey of the Sinai and Levant, with a particular emphasis on the Rift Valley. The team consisted of the geologist Dr. Edward Hull, his son the medical doctor Gordon Hull, who was also the team's photographer, George Armstrong, (formerly Sergeant-Major of the Royal Engineers), who had worked with the PEF on the Survey of Western Palestine, Major Horatio Herbert Kitchener R.E., another veteran of the Western Survey, the naturalist Henry C. Hart, and the meteorologist Reginald Laurence of the Royal College of Science, Dublin. The results of their survey were published in a volume of the 1886 edition of *The Survey of Western Palestine* (Hull 1886), and in a more popular account by Edward Hull (with reports by Kitchener, and Armstrong), entitled *Mount Seir, Sinai and Western Palestine*, published by the PEF in 1885. It is Gordon Hull's photographs from this expedition that illustrate the landscape of the Wadi Arabah in this chapter.

Approaching the Wadi Arabah from the Sinai and Western Palestine, the Haj Road, or the route of the Pilgrimage Caravan to Mecca, has always had prominence amongst the Muslims of the area south of Damascus. The major road through the Sinai was used by the Egyptian Caravan (including the pilgrims of North Africa), whilst a smaller caravan started from Gaza, joining the Sinai route at Aqaba.

The PEF party started their survey of the Wadi Arabah at Aqaba, at the southern end of the rift. There they made arrangements with Sheikh Muhammad Ibn Jad of the Alaween tribe (whom the group nicknamed 'Sheik Shark' in response to his ever-increasing demands for money), who had agreed to take them up the Wadi Arabah (Hull 1885: 67-69).

The Wadi Arabah is a long and narrow depression, with the mountains of both the Sinai and the Negev to the west, and of Edom to the east often in

Fig. 27: This view over the desolate terrain of the northern Sinai was taken by Gordon Hull from the Haj road west of Aqaba, looking down into the Wadi Arabah, with the mountains of Edom in the distance.

These views of the Wadi Arabah show the flat, sandy floor of the valley with the mountains in the distance (Fig: 28: above); the gently undulating scrubland near the watershed (Fig. 29, right); and the rocky landscape looking westwards from the source of Wadi Zelegah towards the lowest scarp of the Tih Plateau (Fig. 30, below right).

plain view. In the winter months enough rain would fall to support the abundant growth of desert shrubs.

In places, the wadi bed supports clusters of shrubs and trees; *retem* (wild broom), *shih*, and tamarisk, and acacia – plants able to survive the harsh conditions and provide nourishment for livestock.

Fig. 31: The bedouin pictured above is attired in a broadly striped abayah, *or cloak, of a type that has since fallen out of fashion with the tribesmen of the Transjordanian countryside. The lighter, usually white, stripe was made of wool, and the darker (brown) section was usually made of camel hair.*

Fig. 32 (left): *Bedouin take their ease in a small wadi east of Wadi Arabah.*

Fig. 33 (below) and Fig. 34 (opposite): Camels and men slake their thirst at the watering hole at 'Ain Ghudian, north of Aqaba.

Forty-eight kilometres north of Aqaba is the site of 'Ain Ghudian, a well-known watering hole situated in a flat and marshy landscape.[2] An intimate knowledge of the various springs and pools which occur in the Wadi Arabah could mean the difference between life and death for the people and animals who made their home here in this seemingly barren land, or used it as a thoroughfare between other areas. There are two wells at 'Ain Ghudian, the larger of which is big enough to accommodate camels, and both of which are

surrounded by a relative profusion of sturdy desert shrubs, evidence of the high water table in the area. The PEF survey party was running low on water by the time they reached these wells five days after departing Aqaba, and their presence at this crucial point was very much appreciated by camels and men alike (Hull 1885: 82-83).

The survey party continued north to the Wadi Ghurundal on the eastern side of the Wadi Arabah, a narrow valley surrounded by high mountains, leading into the heart of the Edomite range. The geology of this area was of particular interest to Edward Hull and his team, being the spot where the main fault line of the Arabah was crossed, which created a spectacular landscape of high cliffs of contrasting sandstones and red porphyries. The complex geology and fault lines in the rocks have given rise to fresh water springs that well up wherever there is a weakness in the rock to be exploited. This abundance of water has led to a particularly rich flora and fauna, as Hull describes:

During the day, when crossing the numerous sand dunes, it helped to pass the time to note the many and varied footprints often clearly impressed on the surface. Of these the most numerous were those of the gazelle, others of hyaenas, and a few of large felines, probably leopards. If one were to draw a conclusion from the great numbers of these footprints it would be that during the night the whole surface of the valley is alive with wild animals, which emerge from their dens and hiding-places in search of food and water. (1885: 83-84).

Fig. 35 (right) *and Fig. 36:* (below) *show views of the Wadi Ghurundal's narrow valley, which leads to the heart of the Edomite range.*

The Wadi Ghurundal is remembered today with fondness by the older generation of Jordanians who talk of the police outpost that was established in it back in the early 1920s. The policemen who manned it, some 20 in all, were especially chosen from the ranks of the Camel Corps. As there were no roads in those days, vehicles could not reach the site and the garrison had to travel from their base at Ma'an, far to the east, to Ghurundal on camel back, a journey of one or two days.

Nearly halfway between Aqaba and the Dead Sea, the PEF survey party came to a point from which they could see the famous Mount Hor (the legendary burial place of Moses' elder brother, Aaron) in the distance, and made camp.

Continuing ever northwards, the expedition came to 'Ain Buweirdeh, sometimes given as 'Ain Abu Werideh. Horatio Kitchener, writing in his report in Hull's *Mount Seir* describes something of the confusion that could arise with regard to the accurate recording of place names in the region:

> It was impossible to find out the exact name, as the Arabs themselves were divided on the subject. I am inclined to think Buweirdeh is the correct name.(Hull 1885: 86-96).

Buweirdeh is the Arabic feminine form of *buweird*, meaning 'the cold', which, in this case, is probably a reference to water.

The PEF survey of the Wadi Arabah came to an end in the Ghor es-Safi, at the southern tip of the Dead Sea, where they made camp before heading

Fig. 37: Behind the survey team's camp, midway betwee Aqaba and the Dead Sea, rises Mount Hor, atop which lies Aaron's Tomb.

west into the Negev desert and to Gaza. The Ghor es-Safi[3] is today a centre of market garden farming, employing deep bore holes to access subterranean water

Fig. 38: A bedouin warrior with his spear and camel stand amid the sand dunes at 'Ain Buweirdeh, on the eastern flank of Wadi Araba. The plentiful water in the area encourages the growth of retem, *or wild broom seen in the background.*

for irrigation. At the end of the nineteenth century, at the time when the photograph below was taken, the area was inhabited by the Ghawarneh tribes. Their means of livelihood were primarily small-scale millet plantations and cattle and goat rearing. Sheep are generally not suited to the heat of the Ghor es-Safi, or of the Jordan Valley to the north.

The Dead Sea itself is in fact a land-locked salt water lake, 80.5 kilometres long, 17.7 kilometres wide and some 417 metres below sea level. The high concentrations of salts and other minerals in the water endow the Dead Sea with its legendary characteristics. When the concentration of these minerals

Fig. 39: The PEF expedition camp at Ghor es-Safi.

reaches saturation point, they begin to solidify and crystallize, showing up as patches of salt on the surface. Sometimes even larger crystalline structures float on the water's surface, looking rather like icebergs. The Dead Sea[4] has a salinity of 3,000 mg/l, and is the saltiest body of water in the world.[5] The salts are partly attributed to mineral springs that occur under the lake bed itself, and on its southern shore. Additional minerals are also carried down to the sea by the waters of the Jordan and its tributaries, such as the Wadi Zarqa which is, in part, fed by mineral springs.

The high concentrations of these minerals and salts are due to an ongoing dual process. Firstly, there is the rapid rate of water evaporation from the

surface of the lake, particularly in summer, when temperatures can regularly reach 40°C or more. In addition, the Dead Sea is the terminus for the Jordan River: there is no outlet into the Wadi Arabah, which rises up back to sea level from the low point of the Dead Sea. Therefore, all the minerals brought down to the Dead Sea by the Jordan River and its tributaries have been continually concentrated over time. As well as sodium chloride, its mineral cocktail includes concentrations of bromides, magnesium and calcium chloride and sulphur. This mixture has made the Dead Sea the site of human activity for many years. At least since Roman times, if not before, the waters have been regarded as beneficial to the health, especially for the skin (although highly

Fig. 40: The view across the Dead Sea, looking westwards towards the mountains of Moab. The areas of white on the surface of the water are concentrations of salt residues created by the movement of the water. (Photochrom Co. 1880-1900.)

poisonous if taken internally). Scratches and insect bites heal very quickly if treated with a dose of Dead Sea water, and a variety of skin conditions are said to respond well to a Dead Sea treatment. Dead Sea beauty products are manufactured in both Israel and Jordan in an attempt to cash in on the extraordinary therapeutic properties of the water and the soil of the area, and spa resorts (both medicinal and more tourist-focused in nature) flourish on both sides. The extraordinary buoyancy that the dissolved minerals produce adds another element of novelty to taking a dip in the Dead Sea.

South of the Lisan peninsula, which juts out from the eastern bank, Israel and Jordan have embarked on intensive chemical extraction processes, creating large expanses of salt pans at its southern end, effectively shrinking the surface area of the lake as the industries expand. In previous years, the salts and boulders of asphalt that float to the surface of the sea have been harvested by local bedouin who, by this means, were able to eke out a living in this inhospitable land.

Just visible in Figure 42 is the Lisan peninsula, a remnant of the seabed of the earlier Lisan Lake that once covered a far larger part of the rift valley than the Dead Sea does today.[6] The water level of the Dead Sea becomes steadily shallower the further south one goes. At the point where the Lisan extends furthest westwards, it can be very shallow indeed, sufficiently so to allow pack animals to make the crossing to the western bank without difficulty, as was observed by Charles Irby and James Mangles in 1818 (1823: 453-454).

Fig. 41: A watercolour by Claude Conder in 1873, painted during the Survey of Western Palestine. It depicts the view southeast over the Dead Sea, looking towards the mountains of Moab.

At the north end of the Dead Sea lies the island of Rujm el-Bahr, the 'Ruin of the Sea'. This island, now absorbed into the ever-advancing shoreline of the Dead Sea and no longer visible, was marked on W. F. Lynch's map of 1848 (1850: sketch map opposite p.268), and on Sheet 18 of the PEF's *Survey of Western Palestine* map published in 1880. On this later map, it is marked as being 390 metres below sea level.

In rough weather, driftwood is washed into the River Jordan and carried down to the Dead Sea by high waves. Deposits form around the mouth of the river, and further down the coast to Swaymeh, an area that has, in recent years, been developed as a tourist resort. Naturally, the occurrences of this debris are greater in years where water levels in the Jordan itself are higher, creating a stronger current and inflow into the Dead Sea. Presently, the volume of water brought by the river has become so diminished that the level in the Dead Sea has dropped alarmingly, a cause of great concern amongst scientists and government offices in Jordan, and its neighbours in the region. Plans are now

Fig. 42: The shore of the Dead Sea, showing the island of Rujm el-Bahr by Bonfils, 1867-1896). In the foreground is a group of three men, one of whom is wearing the distinctive 'abayah.

Fig. 43: Bonfils's view of the north end of the Dead Sea, looking east. In the foreground driftwood lies scattered along the shoreline.

being seriously considered to implement a project that will need essential international support and investment. This is the so-called Red Sea-Dead Sea water canal which will bring water from the Red Sea at Aqaba into the shrinking basin of the lowest sea on the surface of the earth.

The Dead Sea is fed by several significant fresh water tributaries,

THE RIFT VALLEY

including the Wadi Mujib (River Arnon) on the Jordanian side, and most significantly of all, the River Jordan itself. In the Jordan Valley north of the Dead Sea, the climate remains stiflingly hot in summer, although this becomes less extreme the further north one goes. The soils are rich, and with an ample supply of fresh water are now often under cultivation. In antiquity, the combination of a plentiful water supply, and the strategic importance of the location as a trade route made it an ideal place to settle and develop civilization.

On the western side of the river, there are the archaeological remains of Jericho, one of the oldest towns in the world, with a settlement history going back to the eighth millennium BC. Indeed, the whole of the Jordan Valley is dotted with numerous archaeological sites (known as 'tells') with occupation dating back to the earliest times, but with particular significance in the Bronze and Iron Ages of the third through to the mid-first millennia BC.

The Jordan River rises at Banias, at the foot of Mount Hermon, north of Lake Huleh. From there, it makes its way southwards through Lake Huleh, and then to the Sea of Galilee, before making its final descent down to the Dead Sea. It is the section of the valley between the Dead Sea and the Sea of Galilee that we are now concerned with.

Over the centuries, the people of this the Jordan Valley have mingled with the descendents of African slaves who were first brought in to work on the estates that produced sugar cane, citrus fruits, wheat, maize and barley. In the

Fig. 44: A Photochrom portrait of a bedouin family of the Jordan Valley; the modest size of the tent shows them to be an ordinary family. (Photochrom Co. 1880-1900.)

photograph above, the head of the family holds a white mare and carries a long rifle dating to the eighteenth century. Likewise, his seated son carries a rifle, while a second son and a daughter sit behind with their white-bearded grandfather. The circle of stones function as a fireplace, or *nuqra*, as it is called by the bedouin. The fire was used for heating water for tea or brewing coffee, as well as for cooking bread. This last task was reserved for women, and involved turning the dough into thin round loaves which were then stretched over a heated pan called a 'saaj'. The bread itself was called *khubz chrak* and was the basic diet for people in the area in the nineteenth century.

Figure 46 opposite shows the Ghoranyieh ford across the Jordan at Wadi Nuweimeh, near Jericho (now the location of the Allenby Bridge). The various river crossings were essential for all those travelling to Transjordan and the east in one direction, and to Palestine and the west in the other. The photograph was taken during Warren's expedition east of the Jordan in 1867, on 18 July between 8.30 and 10.50 a.m. Writing in the *Quarterly Statement* for 1870, Warren describes the crossing of the river;

> Here was little danger in crossing; for about thirty feet the depth was seven feet or more, and for the remainder it was only two to four feet ...The tents and nearly everything else were left on the mules' backs, but the photograph apparatus and box were put on a horse's back, with a man astride behind, and several on each side, and carried across with much shouting. When we crossed there were two Bedouins on each side, to hold our legs and guide the horse, and it struck me that they did their best to pull us off. Luckily all our horses had manes. (1870: 284-285)

Warren's mules and horses are visible on the eastern bank with tamarisk and acacia trees on the right of the photograph. A group of boys are cooling off in the water. The impressive figure of the bedouin in the foreground, in

Fig. 45: The Ghoranyieh ford across the River Jordan at Wadi Nuweimeh, taken by Phillips in 1867. (Photochrom Co. 1880-1900.)

his white *qumbaz* (long dress) and *shmagh* (head cover) of black and white, is typical of the sheikhs who made it their job during the second half of the nineteenth century to accompany travellers in Transjordan. The lower part of his sword appears clearly, and it is most probable that the revolver holster on his waistline contained a 45 revolver manufactured by Webley and Scott in Birmingham.

The first bridge to be constructed across the River Jordan in modern times was built near Jericho in 1885, some 18 years after it had first been commissioned by the Ottoman administration. Prior to this, travellers had to cross using the fords, or the ferry service which was not always equipped with craft well designed for the task in hand. The bridge, when finally built, was a wooden structure, with a gate at each end for the collection of tolls. The gatekeeper lived in a small hut on the west bank of the bridge.

In the winter of 1891, strong rains swelled the river waters to the extent that the bridge was destroyed. For a long time after that the river could not be crossed except by the old bridge just below the Sea of Galilee, at Jisr el-Majami'. A new bridge was built on a higher level than the old one, with doors at both ends that could be opened by the watchmen and toll-collector. Although greatly damaged by the swollen river in the winter of 1986-7, it was mended and restored (Abujaber 1989: 101-121).

Fig. 46: The wooden bridge over the River Jordan near Jericho, built around 1885. (Mackenzie/Newton, 1910)

THE RIFT VALLEY

Fig. 47: A view across the river looking east. The banks of the Jordan can be as much as 4.5 metres in height, having been cut deeply in places by the strong currents. (Photochrom Co. 1880-1900.)

Pictured below are two views by Phillips (1867) showing the River Jordan and the wider valley, the 'Ghor'. The narrow bed of the river itself, the 'Zor', is up to 46 metres deeper than the surface of the Ghor, and can be anything from 183 metres to up to a kilometre in width. The banks of the river are covered by a dense forest of semi-tropical trees and tangled bush, once home to a rich variety of wild life. The great tenth century Arab poet, Al Mutanabi wrote a poem celebrating a lion hunt that took place in the thick jungles of the

Figs. 48 & 49: Two photographs taken by Phillips in 1867 of the River Jordan; right *the River and the Ghor valley,* below *near Damieh Ford.*

Jordan Valley, and even in the nineteenth century it was home to many wild animals and birds. Today, wild boar are still hunted occasionally, and the region is still a significant haven for birds. Beyond the thick forest of the Zor are the cultivated plains of the Ghor, where market garden agriculture makes it one of the most productive regions of the Levant.

NOTES

1. The depth of the Dead Sea below Sea Level was first established by Captain Charles Wilson R. E., during his survey of Jerusalem for the Ordnance Survey in 1864. The Royal Engineers marked the point from which their level was taken on the northwest shores of the Dead Sea. Since then, perhaps due to Wilson's subsequent close relationship with the PEF, and the PEF's own pioneering surveys in the region, this marker has become commonly, though somewhat erroneously, known as the 'PEF Mark'.

2. The Wadi Arabah does benefit from some winter rains, and in these months, marshy areas and temporary pools appear which can increase the available water supply and vegetation in the area considerably. In addition, the cooler winter temperatures make it a far more pleasant time to travel than in the searing heat of summer.

3. 'Ghor' is the Arabic word for the depression in which both the Dead Sea and the River Jordan lie. The 'Zhor', or 'Zor' is the term used for the narrow channel cut by the Jordan River itself.

4. The Dead Sea was also known as the 'Salt Sea', and as the 'Asphalt Lake', by classical writers. Muslim scholars refer to it as 'Al-Bahr Lut'- the Sea of Lot, and as 'Al-Bahr Usdum' – the Sea of Sodom after the biblical stories connected with the region.

5. See: http://www.livinglakes.org/deadsea for a current account of the Dead Sea and the environmental crisis facing this unique natural feature.

6. During the Late Pleistocene (c.80-60,000-c.13-11,000 BC), the Lisan Lake covered the area now occupied by the Dead Sea, the Jordan River, and the Sea of Galilee. The sedimentary deposits it left behind form the Lisan marl 'bad lands' of the Dead Sea basin and the Jordan Valley. The soil of the Lisan bad lands is entirely barren, bearing poisonous concentrations of the salts and minerals from the ancient lake. These bare hillsides, which can be extensive, especially near the north end of the Dead Sea, appear like a moonscape at various points between the lush vegetation of the river valley and plain. (*See* Macumber 2001 for a summary of the geological and environmental history of Jordan, including the Rift Valley and the Dead Sea regions.)

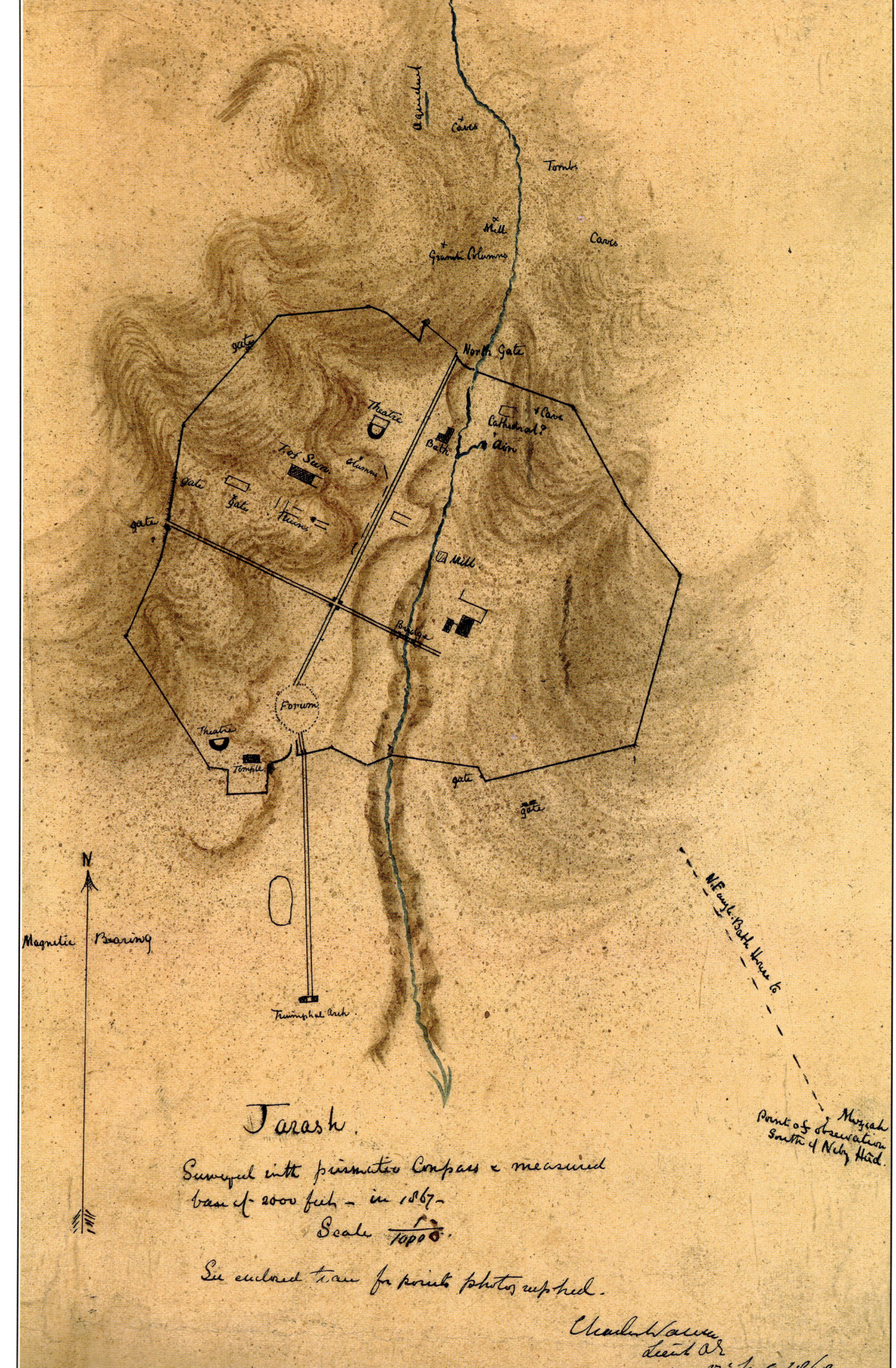

Chapter Four

The North:
Gilead and the Cities of the Decapolis

Fig. 50: Charles Warren's plan of the ruins of Jerash in 1867.

BEYOND THE RIVER

The northern part of the country is rich in archaeological remains dating from the classical and later periods of antiquity. These include some of the cities of the Decapolis – in particular, Arbila (modern Irbid), and Gadara (Umm Qais). Human occupation at Umm Qais goes back as far as the seventh century BC (the Iron Age) (Holm-Nielsen et al. 1989: 598), but Irbid (together with other nearby sites such as Beit Ras) shows a much longer history, with remains dating from the Chalcolithic period of the fourth millennium BC (Bourke 2001: 598). These ancient cities were explored in detail in the latter half of the nineteenth century, particularly by Gottlieb Schumacher. Schumacher was not a great photographer, and left no images of note of these northern Transjordanian sites, but he did produce plans and drawings of some of the standing remains. (Figs. 51 and 52.)

Irbid today is a major modern city, and little remains to be seen of its archaeological heritage. G. Lankaster Harding, a respected British archaeologist writing in 1959, bemoaned the loss of Irbid's heritage: 'The present city is of no particular interest or architectural merit, and the use of

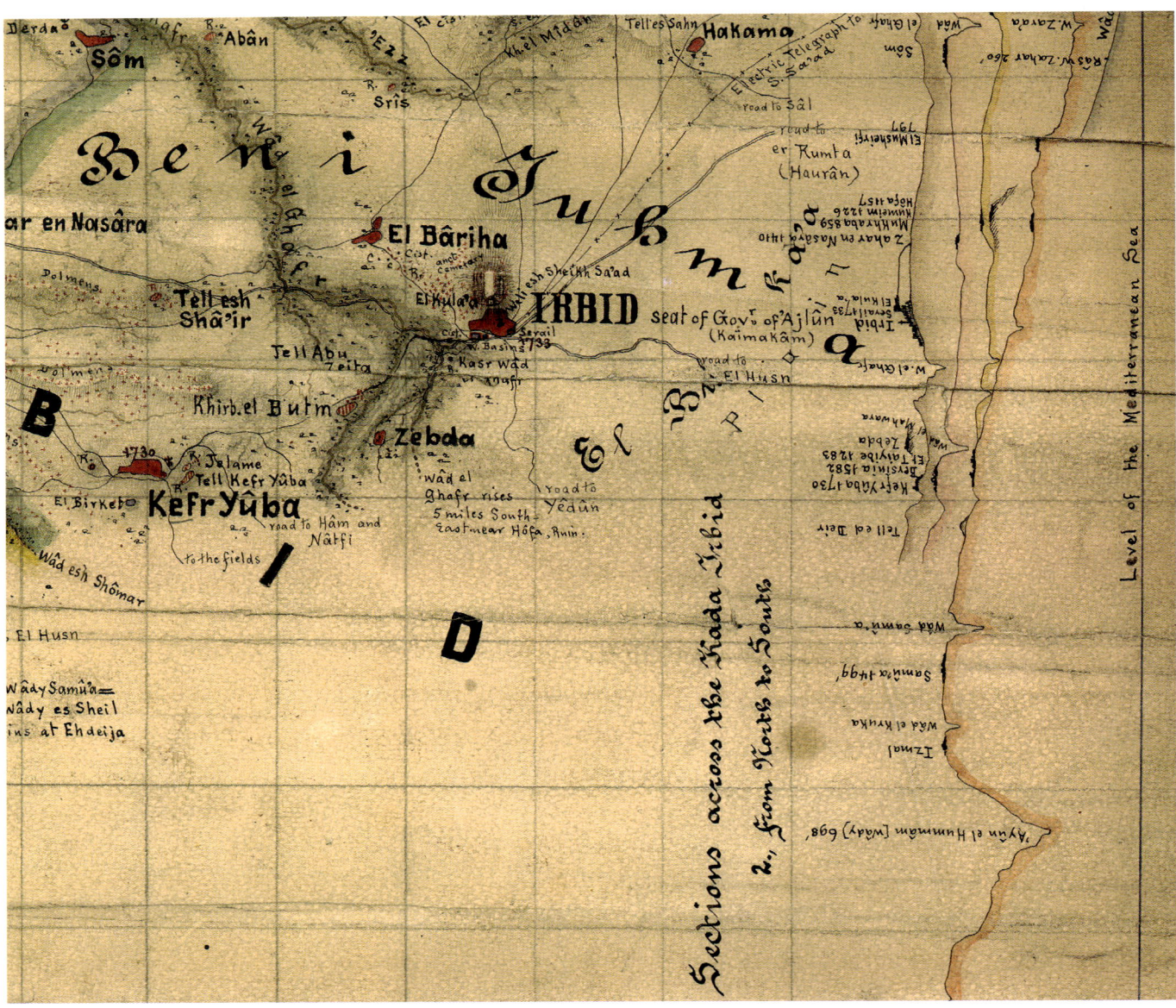

Fig. 51: Part of the original map of northern Transjordan by Gottlieb Schumacher, showing the region of Irbid, 1886.

basalt as a building stone certainly adds no touch of beauty to the scene.' (55-56)

In contrast, Umm Qais has been excavated since 1974 by the German Evangelical Institute of the Archaeology of the Holy Land, which has also undertaken the restoration of much of the ancient town. Modern buildings are almost totally absent, and as a result, it is one of the most unspoilt ancient sites in modern Jordan.

The city of Umm el-Jimal, to the east of Irbid was not a Decapolis member but a Nabataean town that commanded the Eastern route between Petra and Damascus. It is a fine example of a city exhibiting the style of architecture peculiar to towns in the black desert of the Hauran, where the exclusive use of basalt for all building purposes has given them a very special character.

The town was visited by several travellers in the nineteenth century, including the APES in the 1870s and Schumacher in the 1890s. The first major archaeological work was undertaken by the Princeton University Expedition to southern Syria in 1905 and 1909 directed by Howard Crosby Butler (Butler 1913: section A, part 3). More recently, from 1972 to 1995, excavations and studies were directed by Bert de Vries for Calvin College, Grand Rapids, Michigan (*see* de Vries 1997: 276-279 for a summary of the results).

Umm el-Jimal (meaning the 'Mother of Camels') is situated at the foot of an ancient lava flow that comes down from the Jebel Druze. The water supply to the city came almost entirely from winter rains, and was channeled into cavernous cisterns for storage. This water supply, and the rich volcanic soil, meant that agriculture was a very viable occupation for the inhabitants in antiquity.

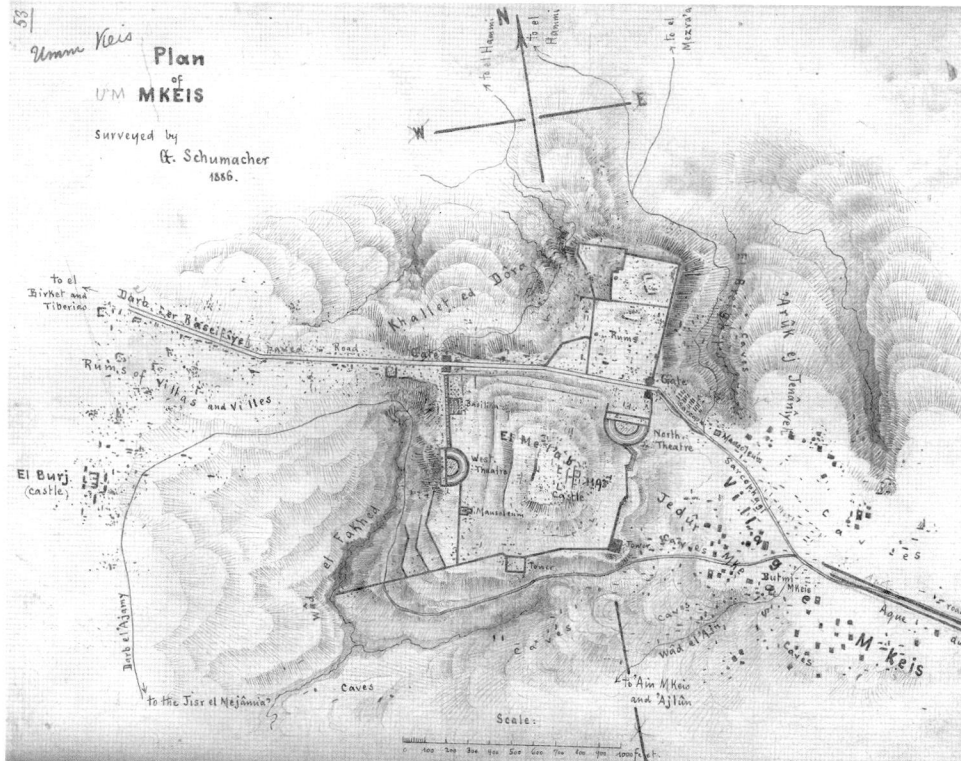

Fig. 52: Original plan of Umm Qais by Schumacher, 1886.

Umm el Jimal was first established in the first century AD as a Nabataean and Roman town. It was an Imperial military town in the third and fourth centuries with barracks and a *praetorium*, but became more civilian and particularly religious in nature in the Byzantine period of the fifth and sixth centuries, with some 15 churches. Umm el-Jimal's ancient name is not precisely known. Initial identifications as the town of Thantia (Butler 1913: 151) have been replaced by suggestions that it might instead be the 'Surattha' mentioned in Ptolemy's *Geographia* (Macadam 1986: 17). The town continued to flourish, but on a slightly smaller scale, in the Umayyad period. It was, however, badly affected by plague and earthquake in the 8th century which led to an abandonment of the town, with only a brief revival as a Druze settlement between 1910 and 1935. The lack of later activity has meant that this extraordinary and evocative site has been wonderfully preserved. It is easily recognizable today as the same town photographed by T. R. Dumas for the APES in the 1870s. (Figs. 53 and 54.)

It is not unusual to see buildings of three or four storeys still standing in the town – centuries after the buildings had been abandoned, a testimony to the durability of the basalt, and the skill of the builders.

The stones of the walls, arches, stairways and roofs are all of this black basalt and it is therefore natural that the town appears like a 'black smear' on the edge of the flat desert plain. 'Five thousand people once lived here. People who knew how to shut out the hostile desert and create comfort even for their animals; people who knew how to channel and store the precious winter rain to slake the summer thirst. People who knew how to coax a crop of grain of the barren desert' (de Vries 1982: 5).

Situated by the banks of the River Chrysohoas (the 'Golden River'), Jerash – or Gerasa as it was known – was a leading city of the Decapolis, and a major city in Rome's eastern empire. Most of the stunning visible archaeological remains reflect its one-time wealth as a Roman and Byzantine city, although increasingly the Hellenistic city is also being uncovered and more fully appreciated. It was under Hadrian (AD 117-138) and the Antonines that Jerash reached its zenith. Hadrian stayed at the city during the winter of AD 129-30, an event that catapulted its international reputation as a major city in the East. Hadrian also bestowed the honorary status of a 'holy and inviolate and autonomous city' on Jerash, which further enhanced its image in the Roman world, bringing great wealth and investment to the city and its people.

A pre-classical settlement certainly existed at Jerash, although remains of this are scanty. The city remained inhabited until the earthquakes of the eighth century AD laid the town to waste. It saw sporadic settlement until the Crusader period, when it was finally destroyed by Baldwin III in AD 1122 (Braemer 1989: 316-337).

In 1878, the modern town was established on the east bank of the Chrysohoas, and within the ancient town walls by Circassian refugees resettled by the Ottoman administration (Browning 1982: 75; Rogan 1999: 73).

Ulrich Jasper Seetzen, the first in modern times to visit the ruins of Jerash in 1806, could not hide his surprise that the city had not been noticed before him. He wrote: 'it is impossible to explain how this place, formerly of such

Opposite top: *Fig. 53: Umm el-Jimal. This photograph, taken by Tancrede R. Dumas for the APES expedition in 1875, shows the church and convent in the south-west suburb of the town.*

Opposite bottom: *Fig. 54: A view of Umm el-Jimal, taken by Dumas in 1875, showing the western side of the town.*

manifest celebrity, can have so long escaped the notice of all lovers of antiquity. Not a single private house remains entire. But on the other hand, I observed several public buildings that were distinguished by a very beautiful style of architecture. I found two superb Theatres, totally built of marble, with columns, niches & c., the whole in good preservation. I also found some palaces and three temples, one of which had a peristyle of twelve grand columns of the Corinthian order, eleven of which were still upright.' (Seetzen 2002: 143-145).

After Seetzen, travellers and explorers flocked to see the famous ruins, but proper archaeological excavations did not begin until 1925, when George Horsfield, on behalf of the Department of Antiquities of Palestine and Transjordan, removed the debris from the West Propylaeum (Braemer 1989: 324). Since then, Jerash has been extensively excavated, and major restoration has been carried ou..t. The city one sees today is, in many respects, quite changed from the one that would have been seen by Seetzen. In addition, the modern town has completely altered the landscape, as well as undermining the integrity of the ancient site itself. As a result, the early photographs of the ruins and the surrounding landscape are doubly valuable.

The photographs taken by Sergeant Henry Phillips R.E. for the PEF in 1867 (*see* page 78 for Warren's accompanying plan), like the collection taken by Dumas a few years later, give an excellent impression of the preservation of the Jerash ruins 135 years ago. One of the most significant is a view of the Hadrianic Arch (Figs. 55 and 56).

This structure was built in AD 129-130 in honour of the Emperor Hadrian during his stay in the city. Lying outside the precincts of the city, it was the first civic monument of the city to be reached by travellers from the south. The triple archway has a wide central arch about 11 meters high, and two narrower and lower openings five meters high. The scale of the archway is indicated by the small figure of a man standing next to the side of the central arch in Fig. 55. An unusual architectural decoration can be seen in the form of a fringe of acanthus leaves on the bases of the round half columns that frame the arches, a feature that most probably originated in Ptolemaic Egypt (Browning 1982: 77). Many of the ruins at Jerash have been badly damaged by earthquakes, and were in a very precarious condition. The Hadrianic Arch in particular was in a dangerous state of preservation, presenting a risk to the public. Over the years, it has received a great deal of attention from the Jordanian Department of Antiquities and is now heavily restored.

Above: *Fig. 55: Jerash: the Hadrianic Arch, photographed by Phillips in 1867.*

Left: *Fig. 56: Photograph of the Hadrianic Arch at Jerash, taken by Dumas in 1875.*

Today, as one moves north from the Hadrianic Arch, the Roman Hippodrome, the scene of thrilling chariot races in Roman times, is clearly visible on the left. This structure has also been largely reconstructed in recent years[1], and was not significantly visible to nineteenth and early twentieth century visitors. As a result, few photographs were taken, and fewer descriptions written before Horsfield began to excavate the area in the 1920s. A similar situation applies to the South or Philadelphia Gate, the main entrance to the city in antiquity.[2]

Once inside the city walls, one soon comes to the famous Forum, or Oval Piazza as it is often called. The form of the Piazza is unique in Roman architecture. It is not symmetrical, and has been deliberately designed thus. It is clear from the plan of the site (*see* Fig. 50) that the Piazza provided an elegant device to correct the orientation of the main colonnaded street, or *cardo* (Figs. 58-60 and 63).

THE NORTH

Fig. 57: Part of a large panorama of the whole of Jerash, taken by T.R. Dumas in 1875. They show the remarkable preservation of the structure at this time, even after the combined ravages of earthquake, war, and abandonment.

Fig. 58: Jerash: view from the south end of the piazza looking northeast toward the main colonnaded street. The Temple of Artemis (then identified by Charles Warren as the Temple of the Sun) is to the left (Phillips, 1867).

BEYOND THE RIVER

Fig. 59: The first part of Dumas' panorama sequence of Jerash, looking northeast towards the Temple of Artemis on the left of the picture. To the east are the hills on which the modern city is built.

Fig. 60: Part of the panorama pictured on page 82-3. The view is taken from west of the colonnaded street towards the East Baths (the arched structure in the middle-distance) (Dumas 1875).

Fig. 61: Dumas' photograph taken in 1875 showing the north-western side of the piazza, with the beginning of the colonnaded street leading off in the background.

Fig. 62: The view of the eastern side of the piazza looking south-east. The Hadrianic Arch is just visible in the background (Phillips 1867).

Fig. 63: The view of the south colonnaded street running from the piazza to the south, with the southernmost Tetrapylon visible in the centre of the photograph (Phillips 1867).

Above: *Fig. 64: the Temple of Zeus at Jerash, taken from the north. (Dumas 1875)*

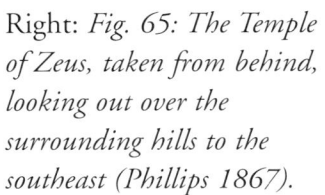

Right: *Fig. 65: The Temple of Zeus, taken from behind, looking out over the surrounding hills to the southeast (Phillips 1867).*

Situated on a hill overlooking the Piazza from the south are two imposing monuments, the Temple of Zeus and the South Theatre.

Two photographs of the Temple, (Figs. 64 and 65) capture the imposing architecture of this important public building, and its commanding position on a hill just within the city walls. Thus situated, the temple would have been visible from most points within the city, and would have been the first dominant structure to greet visitors to Jerash as they entered through the south gate.

Fig. 66: Jerash: the South Theatre, photographed by Phillips in 1867.

Set slightly back from the Temple of Zeus is the South Theatre, the larger of the two theatres at Jerash. In the nineteenth century, before any restoration or excavation was done, this splendid building was in a ruinous state. Today, after many years of work, the theatre is fully functional, and is the venue for a wide variety of entertainments.

The water supply in Jerash was dependent on the River Chrysohoas. The river entered the city near the North Gate and was crossed by three bridges within the city walls.

The south bridge, sometimes called the Pella Bridge, was on the eastern side of the colonnaded street after the South Tetrapylon. In addition to the main central arch, it had two additional arches on each side allowing for the speedy passage of the waters of the swelling river in winter.

Opposite: *Fig. 67: The South Theatre, photographed by Dumas in 1875.*

Below: *Fig. 68: A view of the Pella Bridge at Jerash, looking north, with the East Baths on the left of the picture, and the bare hills of the surrounding countryside stretching into the distance (Phillips 1867).*

Moving northwards from the Oval Piazza, the South Colonnaded Street leads visitors to the South Tetrakionia and Circular Piazza. In the nineteenth century, the devastating effects of powerful earthquakes had left this portion of the street in a ruinous state, with the tumble of columns and other masonry lying discarded in the street itself. Today, the efforts of an international team of architects and archaeologists, working under the direction of the Jordanian Department of Antiquities, have restored this colonnaded street, and other parts of the city, to their former glory.

The Nymphaeum to the west of the south colonnade is described by Ian Browning in his book, *Jerash* as: 'one of the most lavish of all the civic amenities' (1982:143). Built in AD 90, the Nymphaeum is essentially a public water fountain and meeting place, and examples are found all over the Roman world.

The Nymphaeum at Jerash is a prime example of the elaboration of public architecture above and beyond the requirements of its function for the purposes of the beautification of the city, and the pride of its inhabitants. Although relatively small, its decoration is intricate and beautifully executed, and was undoubtedly costly. The niche pediments would originally have been painted and gilded and the niches themselves would have held statues. The lower parts of the structure completely obscured in Phillips' and Dumas' images, were once clad in a fine green *cipollino* marble.

Opposite: *Fig. 69: The view of the south colonnaded street of Jerash, photographed by Dumas in 1875. Even in the ruinous state in which he encountered it, the grandeur of the street is still appreciable.*

Below: *Fig. 70: The Nymphaeum at Jerash, photographed by Phillips in 1867. Even though the structure is half buried in debris, it is possible to make out the rich carvings of the niche pediments.*

Opposite: *Fig. 71: The Nymphaeum at Jerash, photographed by Dumas in 1875.*

Left: *Fig. 72: Photograph by Phillips in 1867 of the ruins of the propylaeum of the Temple of Artemis at Jerash, with the fallen stones and pillars all around. The man standing amongst them looks insignificant in this twelve metre high building.*

Halfway between the South Tetrakionia and North Tetrapylon is the splendid site of the Artemis Temple complex. The complex consisted of a *propylaeum*, which looked on to the colonnaded street, with a series of central steps leading to an outside altar and terrace. A long flight of steps then led up to the east wall of the *temenos* colonnade that enclosed the temple structure itself in the centre of an open courtyard.

The grandeur of the temple, even in ruins, was so dazzling that both Phillips for the PEF and Dumas for the APES spent a great deal of their time carefully recording the details of this stunning monument.

Moving to the northern part of the city, the colonnaded street or *cardo*, which ran the length of the city, continued to the North Gate, and out towards the northern cities of Irbid and the Decapolis.

Fig. 73: The inner façade of the propylaeum of the Temple of Artemis (Phillips 1867). The architectural decoration is seen once again to be finely executed, and every bit as elaborate as that of the exterior.

Fig. 74: This photograph by Phillips of the Temple of Artemis (1867) invokes the solemn grandeur of the temple, standing in the temenos courtyard in isolation from the other buildings of the city. One of the PEF party can just be seen standing on the base of the middle pillar.

Needless to say, the people of this wonderful city had all the entertainment they desired. Their two theatres and the Hippodrome must have provided them with a wide variety of theatrical productions, spectacles, and games to appeal to every conceivable taste of residents and visitors alike.

In its heyday, Jerash was one of the most glorious cities of the Eastern Roman Empire, rivalling even Ephesus and Palmyra in splendour. Despite the ravages of time that befell the city, the early photographers and explorers were undeniably awestruck by what they saw here in a wild and dangerous land. Here was a glimpse of lost prosperity and great civilization close to the limits of explored land; what lay beyond could only be imagined.

NOTES

1. Recently, plans to bring the Hippodrome back into use as an entertainment venue have been proposed, with re-enactments of Roman chariot races and infantry exercises in replica uniforms. Mr Stellan Lind, the proposer of the Jerash Hippodrome Project, kindly provided R.S.Abujaber with this information during a visit on Monday 26 January 2004.

2. Charles Warren marked the depression caused by the Hippodrome on his plan of Jerash in 1867 (see Fig 29), and indicated that it might represent a theatre of some kind in his notes, but no photograph was taken. The South Gate is indicated on the same plan, but not especially noted.

Fig: 75: The Temple of Artemis at Jerash, taken by Dumas, in 1875, shows a close-up of the exterior pillars.

BEYOND THE RIVER

Left: Fig. 76: The view of Jerash from the North Gate, looking northwards, and showing bare hills, free from any modern development, as it appeared to Phillips in 1867. On the small hill on the left of the photograph is the exterior of the North Theatre, a slightly smaller version of the better known South Theatre.

Below: Fig. 77: Dumas' complete Panorama sequence, showing the main ruins of Jerash, taken from the west. (Dumas, 1875)

Chapter Five

The Middle Range: Ammon

Left: *Detail of a photograph taken by Mantell near Hesban in 1881, probably of Sheikh Gublan. (See Fig. 128.)*

Describing his impressions of the Ammon plateau in 1911, Duncan Mackenzie wrote: 'The region around Amman is much more essentially plateau than valley land: It is not hill and dale but tableland and valley. What is distinctive is the upland character of wild moorland and the presence of valleys in the distance is only felt as a more emphatic undulation of the surface where undulations are general. The sense of space and width is everywhere and whatever is confined or narrow is lost as a mere incident in the grand sweep of the russet landscape, stretching far away to the limitless Asiatic horizon' (1911b: 6-7).

This expansive landscape was photographed in 1867 by Corporal Henry Phillips R.E. during the PEF expedition led by Lieutenant Charles Warren R.E. His images not only depict the countryside of the plateau, with nothing more than a scattering of low shrubs, barely covering the limestone strata of the hills, but also show the ruins of Amman (ancient Rabbath Ammon and Philadelphia) situated in a valley surrounded by the hills of the plateau.

Fig. 78: The landscape of the Ammon plateau with the spring-head of the Seil Amman, photographed by Phillips in 1867.

Fig. 79: View of Amman as it was in 1867, photographed by Phillips during the PEF expedition led by Charles Warren.

However barren the landscape seems, this was not the whole picture. Both of Phillips' photographs show the streams that criss-cross the plateau, and gave Rabbath-Amman, the capital of the kingdom of Ammon, its early fame as the city of waters (Mackenzie 1911b: 5). The main watercourse that served the city was the Seil Amman from Ras el-'Ain, a perennial spring, a kilometre southwest of the ancient town. The comparatively plentiful water supply was certainly one of the main reasons for the growth of the ancient city, and for the development of the surrounding plateau as a major grain producing area.

In 1881, Conder characterised the ancient remains of Amman and its environs as follows: 'firstly the prehistoric monuments; second, Hebrew or Ammonite structures; third, Roman; fourth, Byzantine; fifth, Arab. There appear to be no traces of Crusading work but with this exception all the great periods of Syrian architecture are represented at Amman by important remains' (1889: 20).

Whilst our understanding of the ancient history has developed since Conder's day, his study of the ruins of Amman in 1881 for the PEF's *Survey of Eastern Palestine* was one of the first serious attempts to record and describe the monuments of this remote city. Indeed, its remoteness was part of its enduring isolation, as Conder himself noted: 'Amman capital of the sons of Ammon is the later Philadelphia under which name it was known to Ptolemy and Josephus. It was one of the chief cities of the Decapolis. In the fifth century it was an Episcopal city; in consequence however of its secluded position it does not appear prominently in history' (1889: 19).

Despite its later obscurity, Amman was prominent throughout its earlier history. The surrounding area has seen human activity dating back to the Neolithic period (eighth millennium BC). The site of Amman itself was first substantially settled in the Middle Bronze Age (second millennium BC), continuing into the Late Bronze Age (c.1480-1150 BC), although the richest finds from this latter period come from a site near the modern airport, where the remains of a temple have been unearthed. From the ninth century BC, the city was Rabbath Ammon, capital of the Iron Age kingdom of Ammon, the biblical rival of Israel. Despite losing autonomy, the Ammonites retained their distinctive cultural identity throughout the domination of the Assyrian, Babylonian, and Persian Empires, and it was only with the coming of Hellenism that this was to change.

During the fourth century BC, after Alexander's early death in 323 BC, it became part of the new kingdom created by Ptolemy which included Egypt, Palestine, Jordan and Coele-Syria. At this time, Ptolemy's rival, Seleucus, controlled the Satrapy of Babylonia and the northern part of Syria. During the reign of Ptolemy Philadelphus (285-247 BC), the city was given the name of Philadelphia (meaning brotherly love) in his honour. Later, the city was brought under the control of the Seleucid dynasty. Throughout Hellenistic and Roman times, Philadelphia was a leading city of the Decapolis, and became a bishopric in the Byzantine period. After the Roman-Byzantine occupation of the land came to an end in AD 636, it became known as Amman, reverting to its original Semitic name (Dornemann 1997: 98). Presently it is the capital of The Hashemite Kingdom of Jordan and has a population of nearly 1.5 million people, some 50 times the number of its population in its most prosperous days in Graeco-Roman times.

The Bronze and Iron Age monuments that remain are spread around the limits of old Philadelphia. Any that had existed within the perimeter of the Hellenistic city were demolished during the building of the new site.

Fig. 80: Dolmen on the plateau, north-west of Amman, photographed by Mantell in 1881.

Captain Claude Conder R.E. was one of the first western scholars to seriously attempt to research the enigmatic megalithic monuments of the Amman area. His study, which he published in the *Survey of Eastern Palestine* and in *Heth and Moab*, was a comparative study of the Transjordanian monuments in the light of the then current research on the megalithic structures of Europe and the Near East. As such, Conders' analysis was extremely well informed and well researched. He concluded that the dolmens, or 'trilithons' of the Jordanian plateau had never been covered in an earth mound, as was sometimes the case elsewhere, but had always stood proud to the open sky. This observation led him to interpret them as sacrificial altars rather than as tombs. The hollows and channels that he noticed on the flat surface of the 'tables' were interpreted as receptacles for liquids associated with sacrifice and libation. He noted the existence of burials often in close proximity to the dolmens themselves, but did not see any direct structural or functional relationship between the two.[1]

Some 30 years later, Duncan Mackenzie was also very anxious to survey the megalithic monuments of the Amman area, and managed to complete a detailed survey during his trip to Petra with Francis Newton in 1910. His important study, built on the pioneering work of Conder, was published in the first PEF *Annual* (1911b). Mackenzie recorded three main types of monuments; dolmens, cromlechs or menhirs (standings stones which can be solitary or in groups), and circular stone towers known as *malfufs*.

THE MIDDLE RANGE

Left: *Fig. 81: Dolmenic tomb near Amman looking west photographed by Mackenzie or Newton in 1910.*

Below left: *Fig. 82: Dolmen at Rujm el-Malfuf looking east, photographed by Mackenzie or Newton in 1910.*

Below right: *Fig. 82: Dolmen near Amman looking west, photographed by Mackenzie or Newton in 1910.*

By the time of Mackenzie and Newton's study of the Amman Plateau, ideas about the function of these monuments had changed. Mackenzie viewed the dolmens as the earliest remnants of a megalithic culture of uncertain date, and saw their function as entirely sepulchral in nature. This interpretation is one that has stood the test of time, although significant refinements have naturally altered the overall view of the dolmens and other megalithic monuments of the region[2]. Duncan Mackenzie was a keen exponent of a now rejected theory of a pan-Mediterranean megalithic culture that predated the distinctive regional cultures of the Middle and Late Bronze Ages. This theory was still appearing in the archaeological literature up to the 1970s.

Cromlechs, or menhirs, as they are also known[3], are not as common as dolmens. Consisting typically of single rough-hewn stones, they were most likely cultic in nature – places where sacrifices and offerings were made – but a definite interpretation still eludes archaeologists (Fig. 84).

Fig. 84: A cromlech (or menhir) on the plateau north-west of Amman, photographed by Mantell in 1881. This solitary rough-hewn stone is typical of the type found in this region.

The third group of monuments recorded by Mackenzie and Newton were the *malfufs* – circular towers built of regular blocks of stone without mortar, using a dry-stone building technique. Most of these ruins date from the Iron Age, and their purpose is not clearly understood. In certain instances, they might have had a defensive function, but many also appear to have been agricultural compounds, often with substantial residential and administrative buildings attached (Herr and Najjar 2001: 336), suggesting that these megalithic structures were the farmsteads of different groups or tribes who had varying degrees of land ownership, influence and wealth.

There were a few *malfufs* still standing around Amman until the 1960s when the population's speedy growth prompted a building spree that destroyed most of them. The Department of Antiquities, however, managed to save one of the best examples of this type of building. It can be visited on Jebel Amman, next to its Department's headquarters, some 200 metres from the Zahran Palace. The largest *malfuf* so far recorded has a diameter of 22 metres.

Moving forward in time we come to the Hellenistic and Roman city of Philadelphia. The standing remains of this city, whilst not as complete as those of Jerash, are still truly impressive. The grandiose monuments are perhaps even more surprising when one considers that they were built for a population of no more than 30-40,000.

Fig. 85 (above left), *Fig. 86:* (above right) *and Fig. 87* (below) *show the circular megalithic building, or* malfuf, *at Rujm el-Malfuf on the Amman plateau. Many of the* malfufs *had smaller buildings attached, giving credence to the theory that these megalithic buildings were farmsteads rather than purely defensive towers. All were photographed by Mackenzie or Newton in 1910.*

BEYOND THE RIVER

Fig. 88a (above) *and 88b* (below): *Panoramic view of Amman from the citadel, looking southeast. The four-part series of photographs was taken by T.R. Dumas for the APES in 1875.*

The ruins of ancient Amman were first surveyed by Charles Warren in 1867, and a few years later they were recorded in a superb panoramic photograph taken by Tancrede Dumas for the APES in 1875 (Figs. 88a & 88b). This spectacular image shows the whole expanse of the main ruins of ancient Philadelphia, at a time when the only ravages the monuments had suffered were those of time. It serves as a real itinerary of the buildings still preserved to some degree in the nineteenth century, many of which have subsequently disappeared. Today, this area forms the heart of the modern city, and the same view is cluttered with buildings from horizon to horizon. The photograph was taken from the top of the citadel, and looks down into the wadi of Seil Amman. The Odeon is situated on the left side of the panorama, facing the Theatre and its standing colonnade. Further upstream, in a southerly direction, is the bridge across the river, followed by the Nympheum, the only other ancient ruin still standing in the middle of downtown Amman.

To the right of the panorama, in the foreground, are the Citadel (*Kala'h* in Arabic) and its fortifications, crowning the Amman hill, and overlooking the built area in the valley to the south and east. To the north and west is the plateau, which stretches across the river Zarqa as far as Jerash and across the river Jordan to Jerusalem. On the Citadel Hill itself are the scanty remains of the 3-metre wide wall that defended it against many a would-be intruder. Fortunately, the figures in the photograph give a sense of scale, and with a little imagination, it is possible to see how these huge blocks of stone formed part of a mighty defensive structure. Conder described the remains of the citadel as follows:

> The exterior rampart walls of the Kala'h are standing on all sides and at the north-west corner their height is from 30 to 40 feet. They are all built of chaffed stones, averaging about two feet in height and from two feet to four

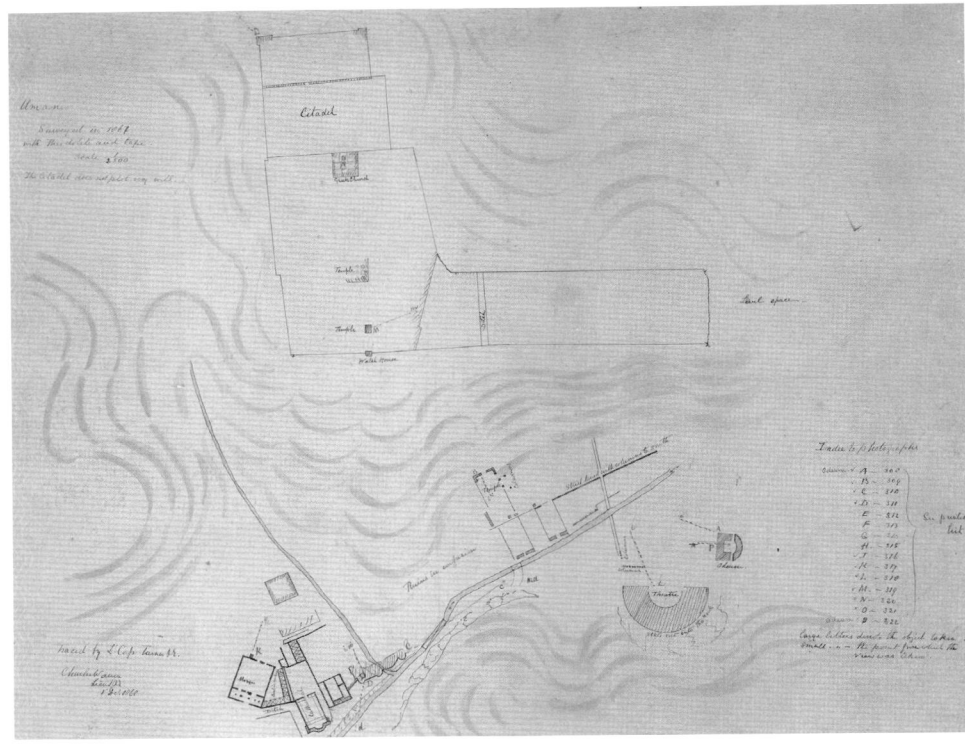

Fig. 89: Original plan of Amman as surveyed by Charles Warren in 1867.

Fig. 90: The façade of the Odeon at Amman, taken by Phillips in 1867.

feet in length. Each course is stepped back from the one beneath about two inches. In the northwest angle, where the hill rises very steeply there are several breaks in the horizontal joint-hires. The masonry may be Roman or Byzantine, but perhaps more probably the former. The longest stones do not exceed 5 feet in length or 3 feet at most in height. The whole area of the Kala'h plateau is thus 1,295,000 square feet or about 29 Acres.' (1889: 30)

THE MIDDLE RANGE

The Odeon, a small covered theatre, standing close to the main Theatre, was obliged, for nearly 60 years, between the 1920s and 1980s, to share its site with the Philadelphia Hotel, established by Thomas Cook & Son in 1922, and for decades the only acceptable hotel in Amman. In the 1980s, the Mayor of Amman expropriated it from its owners, the Nazzal family, and cleared the site for the sake of a more open space around the Theatre and the Odeon. The Odeon, restored by the Department of Antiquities, is now once again in its intended setting after nearly 2,000 years.

Near to the Odeon is the Theatre, carved and built into a natural basin in the hillside, with the repeating seats of the structure appearing to mimic the undulating strata of the limestone rock behind. Writing in 1889, Conder reckoned that the seating capacity of the Theatre was about 3,000 people (page 35). Today, the whole area has been reconstructed and restored, making it the

Fig. 91: This photograph, showing the Colonnaded Street and Theatre in Amman at close quarters, was taken by Phillips in 1867.

Fig. 92: A view by Phillips in 1867 showing the bridge near to the Nympheum at Amman with its central vault intact.

focal point for tourists and Amman's residents alike. The Theatre is now the setting for a wide variety of entertainments, including, most surreally in this sun-baked land, a production of *Holiday on Ice*.

Returning to Dumas' panoramic view (Fig. 88), further along the Seil Amman from the Theatre is a three-arched bridge, one of two that allowed the town people to cross the stream. The second of these bridges was built close to the monumental Nympheum. The remaining arch of this bridge (located at the Muhajireen intersection in the modern city) was still in use until the early 1960s when it was removed, and the stream was covered over in the name of hygiene and road construction. Today, the one-time stream of Amman is Hashimi Street. However, nobody seems to refer to it as such, and it is more commonly known as Saqf es-Seil Street. Evidently, the residents of downtown Amman wish to remind themselves of the running stream that has disappeared completely from their former city of waters, and from their daily life as well.

Fig. 93: This photograph of the Nympheum at Amman was taken by Phillips in 1867 from the direction of the Seil Amman, and shows its outer façade, with the hill of the Citadel in the background.

The last of Amman's major Roman monuments is the Nympheum, another important building which has fortunately been saved, and, like the Theatre and the Odeon, is preserved and maintained by the Department of Antiquities in Amman.

Fig. 94: Photograph by Mantell (1881) showing the interior of the Amman Nympheum.

The Byzantine period of Amman's history was represented by the cathedral. This building, of which the apse was relatively well preserved when it was photographed by Mantell in 1881, had all but disappeared by 1900 (Northedge 1992: 59).

Fig. 95: The Byzantine Cathedral at Amman, photographed by Mantell in 1881.

Past the cathedral, in Dumas' panorama (Fig. 88), can be seen the remains of a large mosque with a square minaret, dating to the seventh and eighth centuries AD. In this period, the tribes of Amman were firm supporters of the ruling Umayyad Caliphs in Damascus, and the city was an important regional administrative and commercial centre. As such, many of the finest buildings in Jordan as a whole belong to this early period of Islamic rule. The Arab historian Al-Muqqadesi describes the mosque as 'beautiful ... with a courtyard laid with mosaics and generally similar to the mosque in Mecca' (1909: 28,155). Conder

Fig. 96: Close-up photograph by Phillips (1867) of the façade of the Umayyad Mosque at Amman

was also impressed by the building when he visited Amman in August 1881, and considered it amongst the most interesting of Amman's Arab remains (1889: 57-59). The site was completely cleared in 1924, when the new Hashemite king, Abdullah I, built the present Husseini Mosque in the downtown area of the city.

Fig. 97: Amman: view by Mantell in 1881, taken from the valley floor, looking up to the Arab citadel on the hill. The fragmentary remains of the splendid propylaeum stand side by side with the meagre huts of the first few Circassian settlers which are just visible to its left.

The principal focus of Amman's Islamic heritage is the Citadel. One of the most interesting buildings here is the Umayyad palace, the reception area (*iwan*) of which was photographed by three successive PEF expeditions – Phillips for Warren in 1867 (Fig. 98), Mantell for Conder in 1881 (Figs. 99-100) and Newton for Mackenzie in 1910 (Figs. 101-102).

The style and date of this building was the subject of much debate from Conder's time onwards. Similarities, both in decorative style, and in architectural structure, were seen with Persian buildings of the Sassanian

Fig. 98: Interior of the iwan *of the Umayyad Palace, Amman, taken by Phillips in 1867.*

Fig. 99 (above) *and Fig. 100* (right) *show the interior of the* iwan *of the Umayyad Palace, Amman, taken by Mantell in 1881.*

Fig. 101: Exterior of the Iwan of the Umayyad Palace, Amman, taken by Mackenzie or Newton in 1910.

Empire of the fifth and sixth centuries AD, the Abbasid period dating from AD 750 onwards, and even Byzantine churches of the twelfth century AD. The building has now been dated to the Umayyad period of the seventh century AD, although its use continued into the Abbasid period. Its plan is that of a courtyard building with four wings extending from a large area in the centre, which has been re-domed in recent years. The façade of this courtyard is elaborately decorated with carved vaulting (Northedege 1992: 75). Fig. 100 shows how the few people living in the area made use of the existing ruins for their shelters.

Fig. 102: Architectural detail from the interior of the iwan of the Umayyad Palace, Amman, taken by Mackenzie or Newton in 1910.

Fig. 103: The Colonnade, Amman, photographed by Mackenzie or Newton in 1910.

With the settlement of Circassian immigrants in 1879, the modern world began, slowly, to make its mark on the ancient city of Philadelphia, and this can clearly be seen in the photographs taken by Mackenzie and Newton during their visit in 1910. The Colonnade, for example, was adapted by the settlers to suit their daily needs. The crude drystone walls built between the columns created a corral for their animals that was bounded by the Colonnade on one side, and the lower stands of the Theatre on the other. Fortunately, this addition was completely removed within 15 years of the date of Mackenzie's visit, and the Colonnade now stands majestically, once more, with only a few scars as evidence of its brief moment of humiliation as an animal pen.

Fig. 104: The Roman Theatre and contemporary village at Amman, photographed by Mackenzie or Newton in 1910.

Fig. 105: This view by Mackenzie or Newton in 1910 shows the full extent of the new settlement, stretching over the hills, with carefully tended orchards and gardens.

The Theatre, too, began to be enveloped by the ever-expanding settlement which soon stretched over the previously barren hills. Gone was the splendid isolation of the view in the nineteenth century as captured by Dumas and Phillips.

Fig. 105: The mausoleum at Qasr en-Nuweijis, to the northeast of Amman, photographed by Mantell in 1881.

Fig. 107: A tower tomb, west of Amman, with an unusually large arched access, perhaps indicative of a ceremonial function. Photographed by Mantell in 1881.

Around the outskirts of the city are the mausolea of the great and the good of Roman Philadelphia, dating mainly from the second and third centuries AD. One of these burial sites, known as el-Khaf or er-Raqim, is a few kilometers southeast of Amman on the road to Sahab. The site is composed of a rock-cut mausoleum which seems to have been used as a burial site until the nineteenth century. A mosque, built in early Islamic times, was still in use when the site was visited by prince Usama bin Mungidh, in 1130 AD (bin-Mungidh 2001: 44). A legend surrounds the tomb, which was recorded by the geographer Al-Mukadasi. A few faithful young men hid in the cave to avoid persecution by heathens. They fell in to a deep sleep that lasted for hundreds of years. When they came back to life they were naturally surprised by the changing world around them. The whole story is related in Surat el-Khaf of the Holy Koran (Al-Abidi 1973: 243). Similar legends exist within Christian mythology, and one in particular, set in Ephesus during the persecution of Christians by the Emperor Decius (AD 408 - 450), shares many of the themes with that of el-Khaf (Velimirovic 1986: 153).

The town of Salt, to the northwest of Amman, in Gilead, was one of the most successful Jordanian towns of the nineteenth century. The photographs taken by Sergeant Phillips, in 1865, capture the essence of life in a provincial Arab town at this time. One of them (Fig. 111), shows the waters of 'Ain Jeddur, a spring famous for its clear running water. This spring still provided water well into the 1940s, not only for domestic and animal use, but enough

THE MIDDLE RANGE

(Above) *Fig. 108: The mausoleum of Qasr es-Seba' photographed by Phillips in 1867.*

Fig. 109: The mausoleum of Qasr es-Sultan, near Amman, photographed by Mantell in 1881, has an elaborate three-arched façade.

BEYOND THE RIVER

Fig. 110: The mausoleum of el-Khaf (er-Raqim) photographed by Mantell in 1881.

to supply a local winery and *'arak* (the local aniseed aperitif) factory as well. When a new water pipe system was later introduced, the spring was harnessed, and its water supply was diverted to the main reservoir of the municipality. This interruption of the spring's flow, led to the immediate closure of the winery. Another of Phillips' images (Fig. 112) provides a panoramic view of the town itself, looking towards the northwest, with its traditional mud-brick flat roofed houses scrambling up the side of the hill. At the top is the castle, known as 'Ras el-Emir' (the Head of the Prince). It was rebuilt during the Crusades in 1189 by El-Mozzam Issa (AD 1182-1227) son of El-Adil (AD 1145-1218), the brother of Saladin (AD 1138-1193) of the Ayyubids. Unfortunately this important monument was removed as a result of a new town plan in 1964.

Fig. 111: The waters of 'Ain Jeddur, a spring near Salt, famous for its clear running water, photographed by Phillips in 1867.

Below: *Fig: 112: Two-part panoramic picture of Salt looking towards the Citadel, taken by Phillips in 1867. In the foreground, in the fertile valley at the foot of the hill, are the orchards and fields that provided the town with its supply of vegetables and fruits, especially grapes and figs for which the area was famous.*

BEYOND THE RIVER

Fig. 113: Dumas' two-part panoramic picture of Salt from the north-west, taken for the APES in 1875.

Fig. 114: The Castle of Salt from the west, taken by Dumas for the APES in 1875.

A few years later, in 1875, Tancrede Dumas took several photographs of Salt for the American Palestine Exploration Society, including a panorama showing the town on either side of the valley, with the orchards and surrounding hills in the distance (see Fig. 113) and an interesting view of the castle after it had been repaired by the Ottoman administration in 1867, shortly before a garrison was stationed there.

Not only did the pleasing aspect of Salt appeal to the early photographers. In 1887, the town was evocatively captured in watercolours by the artist, James Clark R.I. (Fig. 115).

Although better known for his portraits, he was particularly fond of painting landscapes and views of the East, often with biblical themes.

THE MIDDLE RANGE

Fig. 115: Watercolour of Salt by J. Clark, painted in 1887. Clark donated a number of his Near Eastern views to the PEF in 1935, of which this is one. With the evocative title, 'Moonlight Es-Salt', it conjurs up a scene of slumbering tranquillity and security in this small town of Gilead.

Ten kilometres south of Amman, on the road to Madaba, are the ruins of Khirbet es-Suq (meaning 'the ruin of the market-place'), a once prosperous town of 5,000 or so people. Although the ruins were extensive in the nineteenth century, they are now practically obliterated. The only monument worth mentioning these days is the mausoleum on the left of the road from Amman to Madaba. Unfortunately, it has been completely neglected, and is now hemmed in between modern shops and buildings.

THE MIDDLE RANGE

Fig. 116 (top left): The mausoleum of Khirbet es-Suq photographed by Phillips. It shows the eastern façade of the building as it was in 1867. Much of the building lies buried beneath an accumulation of soil, so that only the very top of the structure is visible.

Fig. 117 (bottom left): An interior view of the mausoleum of Khirbet es-Suq photographed by Phillips in 1867, showing a tumble of stones.

Fig. 118 (below): Khirbet es-Suq by Phillips, showing a broad view of the whole site, with the ruins of the town, and the remaining standing columns of the temple as they were in 1867.

Fig. 119: A general view of the site of 'Iraq el-Emir, with a line of massive masonry visible below the summit of the hill. Photographed by Dumas in 1875.

Fig. 120 (below): The palace at 'Iraq el-Emir from the east, showing the south-east corner of the front wall with animals in relief. Photographed by Dumas in 1875.

A site that has fared far better than Khirbet es-Suq is the palatial building, probably a summer residence, at 'Iraq el-Emir, in the Wadi Sir valley between Amman and the Jordan Valley. It was probably built between the years 182-175 BC in the time of Seleucus IV (187-175 BC). In this respect, archaeologists seem to agree with the famous Jewish historian Josephus, who refers to the building in *Antiquities of the Jews* (12, IX, 11). It is generally accepted that the owner was Hyrcanus of the Tobiad dynasty, the grandson of the daughter of a celebrated chief of the Sanhedrin in Alexander the Great's time. After a quarrel with his brothers in Jerusalem, who supported the Seleucid dynasty of Syria, he was banished to Transjordan in about 177 BC, where he began to build this palace (known as Qasr el-'Abed in Arabic) within a wider complex of buildings and defensive walls. However, his grand design was never completed, and the upper storeys of the palace, originally intended to house the private chambers of the owners, remained incompleted. The Qasr el-'Abd was designed to be surrounded by water, appearing to float like a barge in an artificial lake. The lake was fed with water from the surrounding hills, which was brought to the site by way of underground channels. Elaborate lion or panther-shaped fountains then delivered the water to its destination (Schmid 2001: 386).

Fig:. 121 (below): A closer view of the palace at 'Iraq el-Emir itself, and of some of the now weathered relief carvings of lions that decorated the corners of the palace's upper storey. The figures in the photograph provide an excellent scale, showing just how massive this structure was, with some stones measuring six metres in length and three metres in height. Photographed by Phillips in 1867.

BEYOND THE RIVER

Since its 'discovery' by Irby and Mangles in 1823, the purpose of the palace remained a puzzle for many years. Many scholars believed that the structure was a temple, drawing parallels with other sites such as the late Phoenician sanctuary of Ma'abed (a water deity) at Amrit, on the coast of Syria, and the Hellenistic and Roman sanctuary of Pan at Banias at the source of the River Jordan (Conder 1885: 174). In a sense, these observations were not so unbelievable. Certainly, in terms of the position of the structure, at the centre of an artificial lake, there are similarities. The carving of the fountains too, into the shapes of lions or panthers, is very similar to the monument at Amrit in particular. However, recent research into Hellenistic forms of architecture in the Near East has tended to shift the balance towards the identification of the building as a summer residence (Schmid 2001: 386).

By the time of Irby and Mangles' visit, the building was in ruins, and was faithfully recorded in this state by both Phillips in 1867 and Dumas in 1875.

Fig. 122: A view by Phillips (1867) showing the plentiful waters of the perennial spring of 'Ain Hesban, which had been, and remains, the primary source of water for the farmers in the area, and the visiting bedouins alike.

The site of Hesban, southwest of Amman, was one of the main centres of Ammon, although remains from this period are somewhat disturbed by later phases of building on the site. Later, in Islamic times, it became the capital of the Balqa region, which is today defined as the area between the rivers Zarqa and Mujib (Jabbok and Arnon). Hesban's importance as an archaeological site has led to a great deal of activity, especially since 1968, when the Madaba Plains Project was begun by a consortium of American and Canadian colleges.[4]

Warren's expedition visited Hesban in 1867, as did the APES in 1875, and the photographs taken by Phillips and Dumas give a good impression of the site and its surroundings at that time.

As with Amman, the area around Hesban is one of the main sites for dolmens and cromlechs. These were recorded by Conder and his party during the Survey of Western Palestine in 1881. The party was accompanied by the now famous Sheikh Gublan en-Nimer of the Adwan tribe (of whom we have heard numerous tales in previous chapters).

Fig. 123 (above): Two-part panorama taken by Dumas for the APES in 1867 showing the landscape of Hesban. On the hilltop is the Shunet Diyab fort, probably built by Ibrahim Pasha, around AD. 1840. To the right are the remains of a cistern, that might once have been part of a flour mill (Prag 1991: 50-53).

Fig. 124: Dolmen at Hesban photographed by Mantell in 1881.

Fig. 125 (above):*Cromlech west of Hesban, with a member of the 'Adwan tribe, photographed by Mantell in 1881.*

Fig. 126 (right): *Dolmen and 'Adwani near Hesban, photographed by Mantell in 1881.*

Fig. 127 (right): *Dolmen west of Hesban, photographed by Mantell in 1881.*

THE MIDDLE RANGE

NOTES

1. For Conder's full comparative study of megalithic structures, and his analysis of the Dolmens of the Levant, see Conder 1885: 186-275

2. For an up to date summary of the interpretation of standing stones (menhirs) and dolmens, see Philip 2001: 175-176 and 200-202.

3. G. Lankaster Harding describes a menhir as a solitary standing stone (1959: 107), whereas Conder describes the menhir as a 'long stone which is the simplest and perhaps the oldest of human monuments. It is the ancestor of the obelisk' (1885: 197). 'Menhir' in classical Arabic means the place where animals are sacrificed. It is also called *ansab* in Arabic, a word meaning memorial stand.

4. The Madaba Plains Project consists of teams from the following institutions: Andrews University, La Sierra University, Walla Walla College, and Canadian Union College. The excavations and surveys cover a larges area and a number of sites, including Hesban, and Tell el 'Umeiri. R.S. Abujaber. is one of the landowners in the area who has allowed extensive excavations on his property over the course of the project.

Fig. 128: This photograph of a dolmen near Hesban taken by Mantell in 1881 shows a man who, by his general appearance, could be Sheikh Gublan.

Chapter Six

The Plateau:
Madaba and Environs

Fig. 129: A general view of Ma'in by Hornstein (1895) showing the then pristine and rather exotic landscape with its steaming waters and palm trees.

The area south of Amman is a fertile land of rich red soil that receives a relatively high rainfall, especially in winter months. Today, it supports a typically Mediterranean agriculture of cereals, grapes, and olives. In the past, this fertile landscape made it an attractive region in which to settle, and the area boasts the remains of cultures of all eras from the Early Bronze Age to the Islamic.

The most significant centre of the area today is the town of Madaba, about 30 kilometres south of Amman. The modern town was established in 1880 by a group of Arab Christian tribesmen from Kerak who had renounced their Greek Orthodox faith and converted to Catholicism (Abujaber 1989: 217). Built on the hill of the ancient settlement, the new town sprung up quite literally on the ruins of its previous incarnations.

During the Iron Age, Madaba was one of the most important towns of the area, together with Ammon, Hesban, and Diban. It is mentioned on the Mesha Stela, discovered in Diban in 1868, and presently in the Louvre in Paris. During the Roman period, it was a prosperous provincial town, and it continued to be important during Christian times. The many temples and churches erected during these two eras, from the fifth to the early seventh

Fig. 130: General view of Madaba taken in September 1895 by C.A. Hornstein, a schoolteacher from Jerusalem. The new building to the left of the photograph is a church built by the Orthodox Patriarchate. Now the main Orthodox Church in Madaba, this new structure was built directly over the ruins of a previous Byzantine church, in which the remarkable mosaic map was discovered.

Fig. 131: Madaba: remains of a ruined church taken by Frederick Bliss in 1895, published as 'Church No. 2' in his article in the Quarterly Statement *in 1895 (203-235).*

centuries AD, were frequently decorated with outstanding mosaics. The style of mosaic art in Jordan is extremely charming, and scenes of agriculture, plants and animals are common themes.

The most outstanding piece of the mosaicist's art, however, is the famous Madaba Map that adorned the floor of the ruined Church of the Virgin Mary. Dating to the middle of the sixth century AD, it is the earliest known map of the Levant, with its rendition of the geography of the Holy Land and Egypt, from the Phoenician coast to the Nile Delta. Important towns and Christian sites are located with surprising accuracy and remarkable detail, and the map remains a unique document of the Byzantine world. It was first brought to scholarly attention in 1887, when a Latin missionary, Don Biever, made a transcription of the mosaic which he sent to Jerusalem. First Gottlieb Schumacher, and then P. M. Sejourne, drew general plans of the ruins in 1891 and 1892 respectively, and these were updated by Frederick Bliss in 1895. A small chapel had existed on the site of the old Byzantine ruins since 1880, but the foundations of a new permanent church were laid in 1894, directly over the foundations of the sixth century church [1]. The map was drawn again by Deacon Cleophas Kikylides, and more accurately by the Patriarchate's surveyor, George Avanitaki. In 1897, the Franciscan scholars, Lagrange and Vincent, were given permission to study the map, and Father. Germer-Durand was given permission to photograph it. The publication of the drawings and photographs in western journals turned the Madaba Map into a relic of international fame.

Fig. 132: The Madaba Mosaic Map. This composite image was created by combining Germer-Durand's famous photographic prints of the map, acquired for the PEF by Frederick Bliss. Placed together, they give a comprehensive view of the map in its new context.

The story of the discovery and preservation of the Madaba Map[2] remains somewhat controversial. The building of the new town undoubtedly led to the discovery of the map mosaic, and many of the other beautiful mosaics in Madaba. Its development, however, also led to considerable damage to the ancient remains. The construction of the new church over the ruins of the old was most likely intended to present the mosaic to a new generation of the faithful, but for whatever reason, it was irreversibly damaged by the building process[3].

Fig. 133: General view of the 'Inner Palace' at Mushatta taken by Bliss in 1895.

Fig. 134: General view of the interior of the ruined palace at Mushatta taken by Hornstein in 1895.

To the east of Madaba, close to Amman International Airport, is the famous Qasr el-Mushatta (Fig. 133-138). Built by the Persians, during their short occupation of the area between AD 614 and 628, this palace was first visited by Layard in 1840. It was first properly described, however, by Tristram in 1872, who was much taken with the ruin:

> we were astonished at the unexpected magnificence of the ruins, unknown to history, and unnamed on the maps...There is no trace of any town or buildings around it ... It must have stood out on the waste, in solitary grandeur, a marvellous example of the sumptuousness and selfishness of ancient princes ... The richness of the arabesque carvings and their perfect preservation is not equalled even by those of the Alhambra (in Granada, Spain) though in somewhat the same style.' (1873: 197-198)

THE PLATEAU

Fig. 135: The gateway to the palace at Mushatta photographed by Hornstein in 1895.

Fig. 136 (below): *The gateway to the palace at Mushatta, a view by Dumas, taken for the APES in 1875. Sheikh Gublan's standard bearer, holding the mark of his office, stands by the entrance.*

BEYOND THE RIVER

Fig. 137 (above): *A view of one of the towers of the palace at Mushatta by Dumas taken in 1875 on behalf of the APES.*

Fig. 138 (right): *The outer wall of one of the towers of the palace at Mushatta showing the uniquely beautiful carvings of animals and plants that adorned the structure. Photographed by Bliss in 1895.*

Unfortunately, the preservation of this spectacular building has suffered somewhat in the last 130 years. In 1905 the Ottoman Sultan, as a gesture of goodwill to his friend Kaizer Wilhelm II, allowed the carvings to be cut from the exterior of the building and sent to Berlin where they have been exhibited ever since.

Western interest in the Madaba area was deep-rooted because of its association with Old Testament figures. 'Ain Musa, the 'Spring of Moses', situated on Mount Nebo to the northwest of Madaba, is alleged to be the site of the tomb of Moses in the biblical accounts (Figs. 139-142). This was the spot where, according to the Old Testament, Moses, forbidden by God to

Fig. 139: A view by Phillips (1867) showing Mount Nebo in the distance, looking across the plateau hills..

Fig. 140: A distant view (Phillips 1867) of the spring of 'Ain Musa and the ravine through which it flows.

Fig. 141: 'Ain Musa: a closer view by Hornstein (1895) of the waterfall of the spring itself.

Fig. 142: A view of 'Ain Musa taken by Hornstein in 1895 showing the old wall at the mouth of the spring.

enter the Promised Land, viewed the territory into which Joshua would lead the Israelites (Deut 34: 1-12). Currently known as 'Syagha', the site is one of the main tourist destinations in Jordan, not only for its biblical connections, but also for the fabulous mosaics that have been excavated by Franciscan monks since 1933. The site is also famous for its spectacular views over the Jordan Valley and the Dead Sea, 1,066 metres below. On a clear day, it is even possible to see Jerusalem in the mountains on other side of the Dead Sea.

Fig. 143: The hot springs at Ma'in (Zarqa Ma'in) photographed by Hornstein in 1895.

A few miles south of Madaba, the traveller arrives at Ma'in, a spot famous for its therapeutic hot water springs. Better known as Zarqa Ma'in, it has been heavily developed as a spa resort in recent years.

The area around the springs is filled with dolmens and other early stone monuments. Outstanding amongst these is a menhir, known as 'Hajar el-Mansub' (the erected stone). Next to it, and extending over an area of about 1.5 kilometres east and west, and one kilometre north and south, there is the site of Mareighat, a field of menhirs, and at least 150 dolmens. During his

Fig. 144: This photograph by Mackenzie or Newton taken in 1910 shows a large dolmen from the Mareighat field, with two ferocious looking gentlemen crouching next to it, brandishing their weapons. The portal hole of the dolmen is clearly visible.

visit on the Survey of Eastern Palestine, Conder was deeply impressed by the site, and although a thorough survey was not possible, he did publish sketches of five of the most impressive monuments, including Hajar el-Mansub (119: 184-189).

Fig. 145: Roman milestone with Latin inscription near Wadi Walla on the Madaba plateau photographed by Bliss in 1895.

THE PLATEAU

Continuing south, one enters the territory of the clans of the Beni Sakhr tribe who inhabited the Moabite plateau. One of these was the Salaitah clan, photographed by Hornstein in 1895. A photograph taken by Bliss in the same year in the realm of another of the Beni Sakhr clans, the Beni

Fig. 146 Tent of the Salaitah bedouin on the Madaba plateau photographed by Hornstein in 1895.

Fig. 147: View of Diban, taken by Mackenzie or Newton in 1910, looking south-east, and showing both north and south citadels..

149

Fig. 148: The Mesha Stela, or Moabite Stone as it is also known. This image is taken from a postcard produced and sold by the PEF between 1870 and 1900.

Hamida (Fig. 145), is of interest for showing a first century AD Roman milestone which had been placed at the intersection of the Wadi Walla and the Via Nova to Kerak.

Across the Walla, and a short distance before the Mujib River (the biblical River Arnon), one arrives at the mound of Diban, the once proud capital of Mesha, King of Moab, whose history has been immortalized in the so-called 'Mesha Stela', still the single most important document for information relating to the language, religion, geography, and history of Moab (*see* Chapter 2).

NOTES

1. Research into the building of the Madaba church in the archives of the Patriarchate in Jerusalem, undertaken in 1997 by Dr. Yiannis Meimaris, has revealed that the construction of the church started on 2 September 1894. Francis Elias Maroum and his brother Bishara laid the tiles at a cost of 2,792 piasters, manufactured and installed the railings at a cost of 1,853 piasters, and Tannas Daoud Al-Halaby supplied the wooden doors and the windows. All of them were Orthodox Christians of Jerusalem. The stones were supplied by Mahmoud Ibn Muhammad Hammad from Sour Baher near Jerusalem for a total of 20 French gold pounds.

2. For a comprehensive history and account of the Madaba Map, one of the best sources is Piccirillo and Alliata 1998.

3. Writing in the Palestine Exploration Fund *Quarterly Statement* in 1897, the outspoken French archaeologist Charles Clermont-Ganneau described the situation regarding the condition of the Madaba map as follows: 'The mosaic, which by the testimony of four monks was until then almost complete, was partly destroyed to lay the foundations of the church, sacristy, and outbuildings of the mission. The church itself was built without symmetry, that it might agree with the original one. The border of the mosaic, with its Biblical decorations, is now outside it. God knows what these workmen may have destroyed, when we see by the ground-plan of the church that they broke the mosaic to set up a pilaster! The mischief is done. The architect came back and reported that the mosaic did not possess the importance which had been attributed to it.' (1897: 217)

Chapter Seven

The Southern Range: Moab

Fig. 149: A portrait photograph of Sheikh Assuna', a dignitary of the Kerak area, taken by Hornstein in 1895.

Continuing from Diban to the south, the traveller arrives, after a steep decent of the Wadi Mujib, to the river at the bottom of the valley. This famous landmark, often compared to the Colorado River, runs through one of the roughest terrains in the world. In ancient times, it was known as the Arnon River, and was for many centuries the dividing line between the Kingdoms of Moab in the south and Ammon in the north. As is normal at the end of the long dry summer, the water level in the river is fairly low and poses no serious problem to those wishing to cross it, or to follow its course up or downstream. However, in winter, with the coming of the rains, all this can change, and violent flash floods are not uncommon.

Some 25 kilometres southeast of Diban and the Wadi Mujib, is Qasr Bshir. It was built as a *quadriburgia* (a small fort with four projecting towers) around AD 300. Excavations suggest that the site began as a Nabataean fort, and that, in Roman times, it was used as a *praetorium* or the residence of a governor on tour (Kennedy 2000: 140). The name 'qasr', meaning palace in Arabic, gives

Fig. 150: View of the Wadi Mujib taken by Hornstein in September 1895.

the theory a certain strength. The excavations further ascertained that the site had been inhabited during the Ummayad period in the seventh and eighth centuries AD. Qasr Bshir was first discovered in 1895 by Frederick J. Bliss, who described the event in the *Quarterly Statement* of that year:

> Then we rode for about 7 miles over an undulating plain, tempting one to a canter, which I injudiciously attempted, for the treacherous ground is honeycombed with rat-holes, and just before we reached another watchtower my horse went down and I was lamed. So I confess that I did not experience the supposed joy of the discoverer a moment afterwards when on crossing a swelling of the ground, the stately and finely-preserved Roman fort of Qasr Bsher stood out solitary on the featureless plain (223).

Fig. 151 (above): General view of Qasr Bshir taken by Bliss in the spring of 1895 showing the fort as it was first discovered: a solitary monument in a 'featureless plain'.

Fig. 152 (below): The entrance and massive walls of Qasr Bshir photographed by Bliss in 1895.

Fig. 153: A view of the interior of the fort of Qasr Bshir taken by Hornstein in 1895 looking towards the blocked entrance that is also visible on the outside in the previous picture.

Fig. 154: *The Roman gateway at Rabbah looking north (Mackenzie or Newton 1910).*

Fig. 155: A view of the remains of the colonnaded street at Rabbah looking north-east, taken by Mackenzie or Newton in 1910.

A day's journey on foot from Qasr Bshir, about 20 km to the west, are the vast ruins of Rabbah, possibly the site of Iron Age Rabbath Moab, and the city of Areopolis in the Roman period. Duncan Mackenzie and Francis Newton visited the site in 1910, on their way back from a visit to Petra, and recorded all of the major standing remains.

Fig. 156: View of the defensive walls of Rabbah as they appeared when photographed in 1910 by Mackenzie or Newton. The massive stone blocks are almost certainly Roman in date, but not in their original positions. The Roman wall would have been far more soundly and regularly built, and the haphazard arrangement of the stones is indicative of a later date.

Fig. 157: The preparation of a traditional mensaf *in the Majjali encampment at Rabbah, photographed by Mackenzie or Newton in 1910. The cauldron containing the meat (either mutton or goat meat) and the* sharab, *or syrup, is carried by two men, while a third is removing part of the contents to place it in the large* mansaf, *or dish that contains the food.*

Fig. 158: (below left): Sharing a meal in the Majjali encampment at Rabbah, photographed by Mackenzie or Newton in 1910. Some are eating, others wait their turn to enjoy the food, and the host, or one of his family, remains standing to serve.

Fig. 159: (below right): Taking coffee in the Majjali encampment, photographed by Mackenzie or Newton in 1910.

During their stay in the Rabbah area, Mackenzie and Newton stayed with members of the powerful Majjali tribe. Mackenzie, unlike some of the other explorers of his generation, was equally interested in the people who lived in the region as in the ancient ruins and monuments. Amongst other subjects he recorded the progress of a feast in the tents of his hosts, beginning with the preparation of the meal, known as a *mansaf* (still a favourite traditional dish in Jordan), continuing with the men of the tribe in the encampment eating the meal inside the large black tent, or *Beit esh-Sha'ar,* and ending with the tribe taking coffee, which is the traditional ceremonial Arab way to end any such meal. The coffee is always bitter, as no sugar is added. It is, however, enriched by the delicious aroma of the crushed cardamom seeds that are boiled with the coffee. Cardamom is an expensive spice, which until the end of the nineteenth century, was imported from Ceylon and the markets of South East Asia. The successful transplanting of the crop to Kenya and Central and South America meant that the spice became much wore widely available.

Fig. 160: The barley harvest in the region of Rabbah, photographed by Hornstein in 1895. The fellahin are using sickles to reap the ripened crop, which is then bundled ready for threshing near to the village.

The area around Rabbah was also home to settled fellahin, as well as to the nomadic bedouin tribes. In 1895 Hornstein recorded the barley harvest in progress, including measures taken to destroy locusts which were a common and frequent pest that haunted farmers all over Transjordan. These creatures, which strip every plant in their way, causing widespread starvation amongst people and animals, swarmed over the countryside regularly until the 1960s, when pesticide spraying in their breeding zones in Arabia and Africa reduced the devastation to crops and wild plant life.

South of Rabbah, and situated on a high hill, Kerak occupies a strategic position, and a spectacular view of the whole area around it. The city was an important centre during the Iron Age kingdom of Moab, and its importance continued into the Persian period (539-32 BC), when it was an administrative centre. In about 130 BC, Hadrian granted it the status of *polis*, and during the Byzantine era, it was the seat of an Archbishop. In the middle of the seventh century AD it became part of the Arab Province of Southern

Fig. 161: The barley harvest in the region of Rabbah, photographed by Hornstein in 1895. Nine men work frantically to destroy locusts.

Fig. 162: A view taken by Hornstein in 1895 showing Wadi Kerak in the deep valley to the west of the stronghold. Oleander bushes, which produce a stunning display of pink and white flowers, flourish by the side of the stream. Today, the Oleander is one of the most successful and common-place wild shrubs in the Near East, largely due to the fact that it is highly poisonous, and is therefore avoided by the ubiquitous herds of sheep and goats that graze the region.

Jordan, until conquered by the Crusaders in the twelfth century, together with Shobak castle (known at the time as Mont Real). Kerak became infamous for the despotic behaviour of its Crusader lord, Reginald of Chatillon-sur-Marne. Not only was he unspeakably cruel to all who got in his way (it is said that he used to have people thrown off the high battlements of the castle for amusement), but his hubristic nature lead him to dare the unthinkable. He planned the conquest of Mecca and the destruction of the Ka'abah, the holiest shrine in the Islamic world. He had two ships built in pieces, and transported from Kerak to Aqaba by camel. At the Red Sea port, the ships were assembled, and set off on a series of raids on ports in the Gulf of Aqaba and the Red Sea. His expedition was annihilated by Egyptian forces near the holy city of Medina, but somehow he managed to escape and return to Kerak. Eventually, however his crimes caught up with him, and, after the battle of Hittin in 1187, because of the heinous nature of his crimes, he was executed by Saladin himself.

In the nineteenth century, Kerak was the largest population centre in Moab. The city itself was, by the nature of its location, a walled town dominated by the citadel. High upon a hill, at 1,030 metres above sea level, it is surrounded by deep river-cut ravines which, in the rainy season, drain into the Wadi Kerak to the northwest of the citadel. To the west is the Wadi es-Safsafa (river of the willow tree), also known as Wadi el-Franj (River of the Franks), to the north, the Wadi es-Sitt (the lady), and to the east, the Wadi et-Twai.

THE SOUTHERN RANGE

Fig. 163 (left): *A view of Kerak, taken from the hills opposite the stronghold, by Hornstein in 1895, showing the plateau and the city behind.*

Kerak's citadel was built by the Crusaders in AD 1142, and fell to Saladin in AD 1188. The fortifications were rebuilt several times, with a palatial reception hall being added by the Sultan Baybars in AD 1263. Kerak was granted the institutions of a Mamluk city under Sultan Muhammad, when several public buildings were built, including a palace, a *hammam* (public bath), a hospital, a mosque, a *khan* and a *madrasa* (senior Koranic school).

Fig. 164 (below): *View of Wadi Kerak with the citadel in the distance taken by Bliss in 1895. Terraces, on the hills behind, attest to the agricultural prosperity of the region. Until very recently, these terraces supported orchards of figs, pomegranates, olives, apricots and quince trees.*

Fig. 165: A view of the citadel of Kerak taken by Hornstein in 1895.

Of all the photographers to visit the region, it was Hornstein who seems to have been most struck with the castle of Kerak. His images provide a fascinating record of the site as it appeared in 1895.

Fig. 166: The citadel of Kerak: a view of the north wall, with its steep revetments down the side of the hill (Hornstein 1895).

THE SOUTHERN RANGE

Fig. 167: Kerak: a view of the west tower of the citadel (Hornstein 1895).

For over 350 years, Kerak seems to have been a remote and unimportant part of the Ottoman Empire. The Ottomans tried every now and then to collect taxes but with little success. Security levels deteriorated, and less and

Fig. 168: Kerak: a view of the inner courtyard and the residential quarters of the troops in the interior of the castle (Hornstein 1895).

Fig. 169: A view of the Serai, photographed shortly after its construction by Hornstein in 1895.

less agricultural activity took place. The settled population was transformed by these adverse conditions from farmers into pastoralists. As such, they adopted bedouin habits and traditions, and very few of them remained within the walls to the town. According to the oral histories of the Haddadin tribe (Haddadin translates as 'Smiths'), their ancestors were completely nomadic for some 200 years before their eventual migration to Ma'in at the end of the nineteenth century (Khalaf and Haddadin 1992: 40). During the occupation of Syria in 1831 by the Egyptian forces, under Ibrahim Pasha, the town fell under Egyptian control. The local population resisted, however, much to the fury of Ibrahim Pasha. He ordered the destruction of the castle and the town, an act of vandalism that has left an indelible scar on the face of both, despite attempts to restore the buildings to something of their former glory.

Travel in the hills of Moab was a real adventure until the end of the nineteenth century. The unfortunate experiences of Sir Gray Hill at the hands of the Majjali sheikhs in 1890 have already been recounted (see Chapter 1), and it is possible that this incident led to the imposition of direct state rule from Damascus over the region in 1893.

During his stay in Kerak, Hornstein took a portrait photograph of a dignitary of the Kerak area, Sheikh Khalil Assuna' (see Fig. 149). This gentleman seems to have had good relations with the missionary William Lethaby, who lived in Kerak between 1886 and 1895. There are two photos of Sheikh Khalil and his family in the book that was written as a record of this missionary's adventure (Durley 1910: 230-255). The sheikh is also mentioned by Sir Gray Hill in his account of his travels:

> In Madaba we were received by Khalil Asunna', the Sheikh (a very fine and benevolent looking man of about fifty five years of age), who a few years ago having withdrawn from Kerak bought a large quantity of land and attracted a number of Christians to the neighborhood. The inhabitants can now muster four hundred horsemen and are able to hold their own against beduin attacks. (1891: 244).

Fig. 170: 'Noah's Tomb', Kerak, photographed by Hornstein in 1895. The strips of fabric tied to poles are indicative of prayers and wishes, left by local people needful of divine intervention in their lives.

With the imposition of direct rule, new civic buildings began to spring up in Kerak. They included a government house (or *Serai*), a prison, a hospital, and a school. The stones for all these buildings tended to be taken from the ruins of the old citadel and town, damaging even further the already badly mistreated buildings of the Crusaders, Saladin, and the Mamluks.

Another monument recorded by Hornstein in Kerak was the so-called tomb of Noah (more likely the tomb of a local sheikh or holy person of less biblical lineage, and far less ancient vintage). The neglected appearance of the

Fig. 171: The west gate at Lejjun showing its huge blocks of stone, some of which are nearly 2 metres high, photographed by Hornstein in 1895.

shrine and its surroundings apparent in his photograph (Fig. 170) cannot but reveal the lack of care and attention that the people of Kerak attached to Noah and his legacy during the nineteenth century.

About 15 kilometres east of Kerak, is the site of Lejjun, a Roman fort that served as the base for a legion of the Roman army, (hence its modern Arabic name). Built next to Khirbet el-Fityan, a substantially walled Early Bronze Age town, the site consists of the Roman fort as well as an Ottoman barracks. Extensive excavations during the last two decades, especially by the archaeologist, S.T. Parker, have revealed what is probably the most important Roman military site in Jordan. Rectangular in shape, it is 247 metres in length by 190 metres in width. 24 massive two-storey towers strengthened the casemate built defensive walls that were nearly 2.5 metres thick (Parker 1995: 258) [1]. Both Bliss and Hornstein visited the site in 1895, but the site was then very much a ruin.

The Roman temple at Dhat Ras, about 20 km south of Kerak, was probably built in the second or third century AD, when the Roman Empire in the east was at its zenith. Although small, this temple was impressive and rather well preserved.

At the southern end of the Plateau of Moab lies the area of the Sharah, a mountainous range that stretches all the way to Shobak, or Mont Real as it is also known. The town of Tafileh is the main population centre in this area, and was the site of the only set battle fought by T.E. Lawrence and his Arab comrades during the Arab Revolt against the Turks in 1917. The town was always well populated. In the sixteenth century, it had a population of over 600 families, the largest in the district. The area is fertile, with no less than 8 springs in the vicinity, and the town is surrounded with olive trees and fruit orchards, giving it a continuing reputation as one of the most beautifully

Fig. 172: The Roman temple at Dhat Ras, photographed by Hornstein in 1895. The site is also known as 'Qasr el-Bint', or the 'Palace of the Girl'.

situated towns in the country. It further has a commanding position, and affords a wonderful view of the valley going all the way down to the Dead Sea.

NOTES

1. 'Casemate' is a form of constructing very strong, thick walls with the minimum of effort or expenditure in time or labour. A wall constructed in this manner consists of two carefully built exterior walls of finished masonry running in parallel, divided into compartments which are then filled with stone rubble.

Fig. 173: A photograph by Hornstein, taken in 1895, showing the town of Tafileh situated on a hill, with the well tended fields spreading out on the lower slope and the valley below.

Chapter Eight
The South:
Edom and the Nabatean Realm

Fig. 174: A photograph by Hornstein (1895) showing the first glimpse from the Siq of the extraordinary 'Treasury of the Pharaoh', or 'Khazneh Faroun' as it is known.

BEYOND THE RIVER

Travelling ever southwards, one enters the region of Edom, meaning 'red' in the Semitic languages. Biblical tradition holds that this was the realm to which red-haired Esau, the banished brother of Jacob, settled after having lost his father's blessing through the trickery of his younger brother (Gen. 27:1-40; 36:1-43). The small kingdom of Edom was one of the three Iron Age kingdoms of modern-day Jordan, along with Ammon and Moab to the north. In recent years, many archaeological remains of the Edomites and their predecessors have been uncovered, but they were unknown in the nineteenth and early twentieth century. However, the Edomites were not the only people to leave their mark on this apparently dry and distant land.

A surviving relic of the Crusader period is the stronghold of Shobak castle, also known as Mont Real. During the last years of the eighteenth century, many of Shobak's residents, Moslem and Christian alike, grew weary of the frequent bedouin incursions, and migrated westwards to Palestine, where they settled in Ramallah and el-Bireh, north of Jerusalem. The area of Shobak then

Fig. 175: A general view of the walls of Shobak with orchards in the foreground, photographed by Hornstein in 1895. A black tent nestles in one of the stone walled enclosures.

170

fell into neglect, a state of affairs reflected in the photographs taken by Hornstein during his visit to the site in 1895. Only in places could be seen the remnants of tended groves of trees suggestive of a more settled and well-tended past. Shobak's fortunes have since recovered, and the area is once again famous for its apple trees that need the sharp winter frosts of the area to bear fruit.

Moving south-east, and halfway between Shobak and Ma'an, the traveller arrives at Udruh, 15 kilometres to the east of Petra. According to David Kennedy (2000: 169), this site is one of the two largest military structures in Jordan. It is strikingly similar in detail to that at Lejjun and of an identical size. The type is similar to contemporary Roman military structures at Luxor and

Fig. 176 (above): *This photograph, taken by Hornstein in 1895, shows the ruins of the once-large church of Shobak castle. The unimpressive structure in the foreground has been constructed from stones from the castle as a domestic dwelling to protect the inhabitants from the bitter winter weather, for which the area is famous.*

Fig. 177 (left): *by Duncan Mackenzie or Francis Newton in 1910, this view of the fortress of Udruh shows the massive north wall which was three metres thick, and still stands at six metres high in places.*

Fig. 178: Udruh; a view of the arched chamber in the principia, or headquarters, of the fortress, photographed by Mackenzie or Newton in 1910.

Fig. 179: General view by Hornstein (1895) of Ma'an el-Kebir, with the walls of Ma'an esh-Shamieh visible in the background on the hill.

Qarun in Egypt. The overall dimensions attest to the importance of the fortress, which was built in the early second century AD. The site continued into the Byzantine period (a church was constructed just beyond the south east tower) and was still in use in the Ottoman period, when a small fort was built within the walls to the west of the main gate.

Ma'an was, for many years, an important market town on the pilgrimage

THE SOUTH

Fig. 180: A view taken by Hornstein in 1895 showing the main gate of Ma'an el-Kebir. This was the older of the two parts of the town.

caravan route to Mecca. The construction of the new Hejaz railway at the beginning of the twentieth century brought even more pilgrims to Ma'an, which had its own station. Together with the Aqaba area, it was part of the Kingdom of Hejaz until this northern part of the Arabian kingdom was ceded to Transjordan on 5 June 1925.

Built around an oasis, in the dry and barren sandstone plateau, Ma'an was

Fig. 181: The walls of Ma'an esh-Shamieh, photographed by Hornstein in 1895.

divided, until 50 years ago, into Ma'an el-Hejazieh (also known as Ma'an el-Kebir, meaning 'the large one'), and Ma'an esh-Shamieh. When Hornstein visited Ma'an in 1895, he recorded the verdant and well-tended gardens of the town, evidence of both the town's location at an oasis, and of the civic pride of its inhabitants at this time. Hornstein photographed both parts of the town – Ma'an el-Kebir, the older part and Ma'an esh-Shamieh, the newer part which had been settled by families from Damascus (Figs. 179-181). Both were originally built primarily of sun baked mud-brick with plaster rendering, and Hornstein's photographs remind us of what many towns all over the Middle East would have been like before the arrival of concrete, which has obliterated the soft contours of the traditional mud-brick buildings, and changed the aspect of the landscape irreversibly.

Travelling west from Ma'an, the landscape changes dramatically. The broad sandstone plateau is replaced with dramatic mountains of Nubian sandstone, the extraordinary multi-coloured rock of the Edomite Range.

Fig. 182: A view across the mountains of Edom and Petra from the east, taken by Frank Mason Good in 1866-7.

THE SOUTH

Fig. 183: This view by Hornstein (1895) shows the village of Elgi, surrounded by orchards and terraces, and high hills to the east. The villagers' simple houses of stone and mud cluster together in the valley.

Moving close to Petra, the traveller would come to the village of Elgi, the largest village in the area which, in Burckhardt's time, was home to around 300 families of the Laythneh tribe (Burckhardt 1822: 423). It was, and remains, the principal settlement in Wadi Musa, and its water supply, 'Ain Musa, was a copious spring that gushed forth from under a rock at the eastern end of the wadi. Elgi was a prosperous agricultural area with irrigated fields and orchards around its outskirts.

Just to the north of Petra is the site of Beidha, or 'Little Petra', a 350 metre-long gorge (the Siq el-Barid) containing Nabataean tombs, caravan dwellings and monuments. It was comprehensively photographed by Hornstein in 1895. At the time of his visit in September, there was water in the stream bed of the gorge, as there must have been on occasion at the time when the tombs themselves were constructed;

At 9.40 we reached 'Ain el-Beidah, a stream of clear, cold water which runs right across the road. Here we stopped for a few minutes to water our horses, and watched the shepherds giving their flocks a drink. (Hornstein 1898: 94-103)

Fig. 184: General view of Beidha showing the rough terrain of the area (Hornstein 1895)

When Hornstein visited Beidha, only the Nabataean monuments were known, but in the 1950s, an important early Neolithic village was discovered opposite to the entrance of the Siq el-Barid, by the British archaeologist, Diana Kirkbride. The site was subsequently excavated by Kirkbride, with the aid of local Bedouins, over the next ten years. The extraordinarily well preserved remains of this seventh millennium BC stone-built farming village can be visited today (see Byrd 1997 and associated references for details on the excavations).

The region of Edom, the southernmost part of Transjordan, is dominated by one site, arguably the single most important and extraordinary

Fig. 185: Façade of a Nabataean rock-cut tomb at Beidha, photographed by Hornstein in 1895.

archaeological site in the whole of Jordan. Since its decline in the sixth century, after nearly 700 years of urban splendour, Petra (the Greek word for 'rock'), and Edom as a whole, had, for many centuries been a forgotten area of relative safety for its inhabitants. This was to change with the rediscovery of the Nabataean capital by Burckhardt in 1812, which transformed Petra into an icon of the romantic era, the 'rose-red city half as old as time' of Dean Burgon's famous poem.

The Nabataeans are first mentioned in 312 BC, in the reports of Diodorus of Sicily of the growing rivalry between the Ptolemies of Egypt, and the Seleucids of Syria, following the death of Alexander the Great in 323 BC. They

Fig. 186: Monumental façade of a rock-cut tomb at Beidha (Hornstein 1895).

were a nomadic group, possibly from the north-east of the Arabian Peninsula, who, some time in the middle of the first millennium BC, began their migration west to the Edomite Kingdom where they gradually settled at various sites, including Petra[1]. Their arrival seems to have been a protracted affair, in which they gradually integrated with the Edomites, whom their chronicles classify as their cousins. The alleged close relationship between the two groups is based on the traditions of biblical legend. The Edomites claimed descent from Bashemath, while the Nabataeans claimed descent from her sister Nabaioth. Both sisters were the wives of Esau, the father of the Edomites, and daughters of Ishmael, the father of the Arabs.

The Nabataeans were masters of the trade in spices from South Arabia and the East to the markets of the Hellenistic West, and they became famously wealthy from their expertise. Their main concern, when their kingdom was established, was to keep the lanes of international commerce safe and open. It was this realization, on their part, that it was far more profitable to organize the free passage of goods than to block it (since traders were always willing to pay well for free and safe passage) that enabled them to become one of the most successful peoples of the ancient world.

Even so, their history is peppered with turbulent events. They were the subjects of unwanted military attention in 312 BC, when the Seleucid ruler, Antigonus 'the one-eyed', attempted to deprive the Ptolemies of Egypt of the benefits of the Red Sea trade routes. The independent Nabataeans, occupying,

Fig. 187: A photograph by Hornstein (1895) showing a dedicatory monument carved into the rock at Beidha, beneath which is just visible an inscription in Nabataean script dating to the first century BC.

as they did, a crucial role in the region's trade, were, of course, a prime target. The Seleucid commander-in-chief, Athanaeus, attacked Petra at night when all the fighting men were absent from the city. The Greek army was initially successful, but after withdrawing from the city, they were hunted down and overtaken by the fighting men of Petra. The battle that followed was a total victory for the Nabataeans, who massacred the invading forces, and regained their property as well as that of the Greeks. In the year 90 BC, the Nabataean king, Obodas I, defeated the Hasmonean ruler of Palestine, Alexander Janaeaus, and recovered Moab and Gilead, which Alexander had previously captured. Aretas III, the son of Obodas I, extended the Nabataean kingdom as far north as Damascus. Pompey sent an expedition against Petra, under General Scauras, but the Nabataeans managed, as in a previous case under Demetrius, to buy him off, and continued to prosper as an independent kingdom.

It was during the reign of king Malchus I, in 56 BC, that a period of political instability and military failures began. In the year 40 BC, Malchus sided with the Parthians against Rome, and the Nabataeans had to pay tribute to Rome when their new allies were defeated. Mark Antony gave Cleopatra a large part of Arabia, including the Nabataean realm, and Malchus was compelled to pay tribute to her. When his payments were not made in time, Cleopatra, with her ally, Herod the Great, launched an attack against the Nabataean kingdom, but the Nabataeans managed to stand their ground. A few years later, however, Herod tried again, and this time

Fig. 188: The Siq el-Barid (or Wadi el-Barid) at Beidha, with the ruins of Nabataean monuments on either side (Hornstein 1895).

he successfully annexed part of the Nabataean territory for himself. During the reign of Obodas III (23-9 BC), the emperor Augustus planned an expedition, with Syllaeus, the chief minister of Obodas, as its guide. A very sly political manipulator, Syllaeus managed to lead the expedition through the most arid and desolate land, so that many of its members died of thirst and exhaustion. The Nabataean kingdom was not yet ready to relinquish its independence. King Aretas IV, who reigned from 9 BC to AD 40, played a part in the plots and schemes between the Herods, and Caesar. Herod Antipas married Caesar's daughter, and then wanted to divorce her so as to marry his brother's wife, Herodias. War was declared, and Herod was defeated. There followed the affair of Salome, and the beheading of John the Baptist, at the fortress of Machaerus, in the hills overlooking the Dead Sea on its eastern shore.

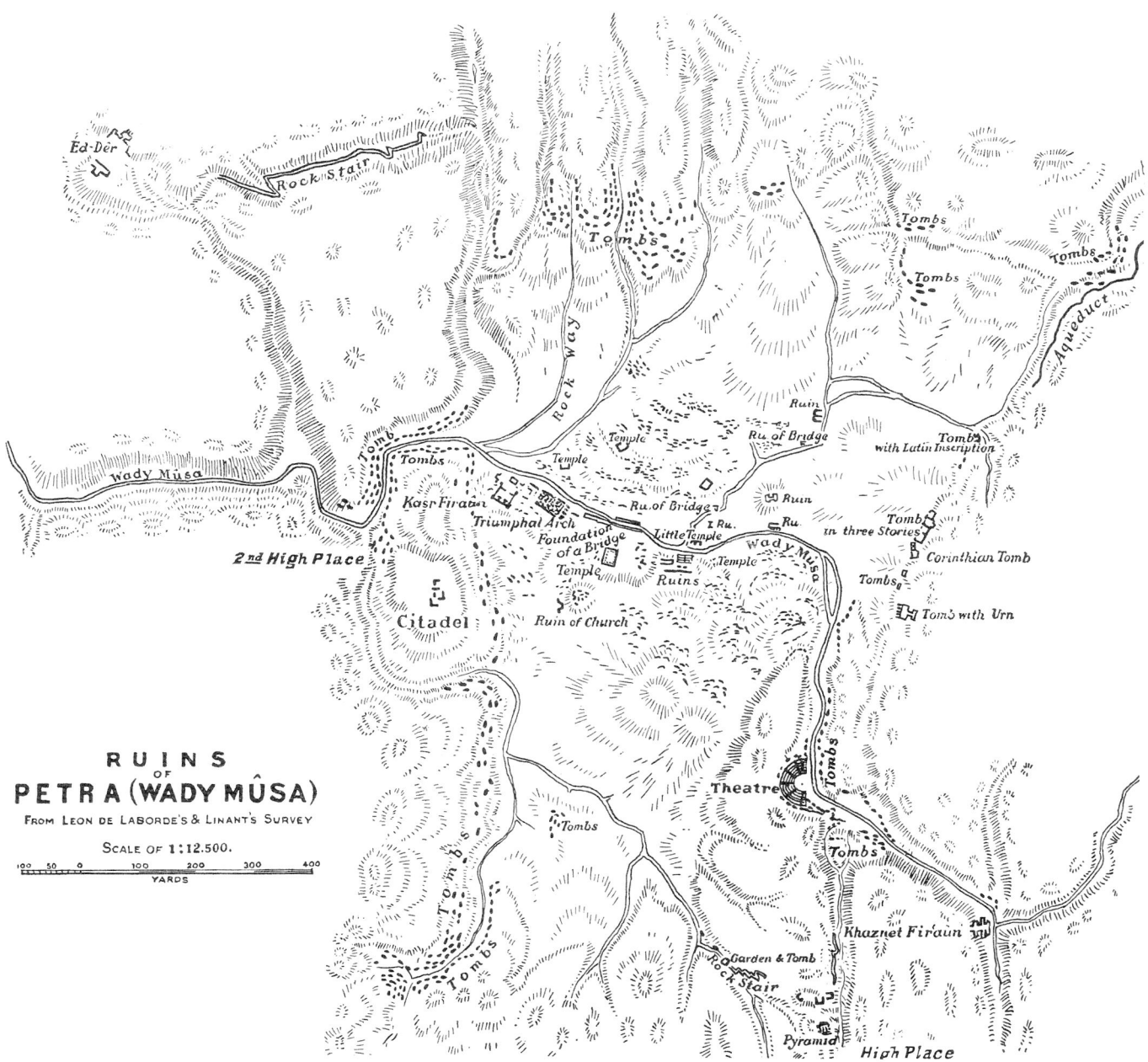

Fig. 189: Laborde and Linat's plan of Petra as published by Libby & Hoskins in The Jordan Valley and Petra *in 1905.*

Following Burckhardt's visit, Petra became increasingly known, and by the end of the nineteenth century it was one of the most extensively photographed sites in the Middle East. The images reproduced here represent but a small selection from the archives of the Palestine Exploration Fund. For the following discussion, the reader is referred to the map produced by Laborde and Linat during their visit to Petra in 1828.

Beginning with the Wadi Musa (the River of Moses), the wadi begins just above the village of Elgi at 'Ain Musa, and runs all the way to the Wadi Arabah. Its channel forms the main route through Petra itself. The first part of the wadi is sometimes known as the 'Outer Siq'. Along this wider part of the route can be seen the Tomb of the Obelisks, and other monuments, including the so-called 'Djin' blocks, which are usually interpreted as tombs (Browning 1989: 110).

Fig. 190: Part of the Wadi Musa (the River of Moses) at Petra, photographed by Hornstein in 1895.

After a short while, the visitor reaches the entrance to the Siq, the narrow passage that leads to the city itself. At its entrance the nineteenth century traveller would have seen an arch spanning an impossibly high ravine. This bridge was described by Burckhardt, as he saw it in 1812:

> About fifty paces below the entrance to the Syk a bridge of one arch thrown over the top of the chasm is still entire; immediately below it, on both sides are large niches worked in the rock, with elegant sculptures, destined probably for the reception of statues. Some remains of antiquities might perhaps be found

Fig. 191: A view of the so-called 'Djin blocks' at Petra, photographed by Mackenzie or Newton in 1910.

on the top of the rocks near the bridge; but my guide assured me that notwithstanding repeated endeavours had been made, nobody had ever been able to climb up the rocks to the bridge, which was therefore unanimously declared to be the work of the Djan or evil genii. (1822: 423)

The bridge was painted by David Roberts in 1839, and was photographed by Frank Mason Good for Francis Frith in 1866-7. This photograph (shown above) is an important record of the arch, which must have collapsed in the late nineteenth century. Unlike Roberts' paintings (which although beautiful and evocative, are sometimes prone to artistic interpretation), the photograph provides a completely accurate record of the appearance of this awe-inspiring arch as it appeared before its collapse. Today, the springs of the arch, and the weather worn niches below, are far more accessible to the modern visitor than they were to the nineteenth century travellers who marvelled at its construction so high

Fig. 192: View of the arch over the Great Ravine at Petra, photographed by Frank Mason Good in 1866-7.

Fig. 193: The entrance to the Siq at Petra, photographed by Hornstein in 1895.

above what was then ground level. This is due to the modern rebuilding of the adjacent ancient dam that diverted floodwater away from the city, and raised the ground level entering the Siq to much as it was in antiquity. Now the arch springs only nine metres above the ground, still impressive, but hardly the work of evil genies.

The Siq is the mysterious, winding passage through the rocks that leads to the fabled rock-carved city which lies concealed from view on the other side. When Hornstein visited Petra in 1895, the entrance to the Siq was completely overgrown, with no hint of the wonders that would greet the expectant traveller at its end. The passage itself has recently been the subject of a large-scale project of clearance and levelling, which has made the access to the site far easier, and has also revealed the Siq's own fascinating archaeology.[2]

THE SOUTH

Fig. 194: This photograph was taken in 1907 by Archibald C. Dickie, one of the PEF's explorers in Palestine. It shows a view from inside the Siq, at one of its narrowest points, with the intense sunlight struggling to reach the ground through the sheer high cliffs. (PEF/P/DICKIE/3)

Fig. 195: A view of the front of the Khazneh at Petra, with one of its pillars (the only parts of the structure to be built rather than carved) missing, having fallen some time before (Hornstein, 1895).

Beyond the Siq the next sight to greet the traveller is truly awesome. Suddenly, after nearly 900 metres of narrow and shadowed passageway, one bursts into full dazzling light, and is confronted with a full view of the Khazneh, a sight that never fails to strike awe and wonder into the visitor. This iconic monument is arguably the most elegant and refined of all the tombs and structures in Petra. As with many of the tombs, it is not a building as such, but is carved out of the Nubian sandstone itself. It was probably constructed in the first century BC, during the reign of one of the last kings of Petra. This was possibly Aretas III Philhellen, who reigned between 84 and 56 BC, when the Nabataeans' wealth and influence were at their height, and the kingdom stretched from Medain Saleh in the south to Damascus in the north (Browning 1989: 91). The strong Hellenistic style of the façade reflects a growing and profound Ptolemeic influence over the architecture and funerary culture of parts of the Levant at this time. Recent work on the monuments of Petra, including the Khazneh,

Fig. 196: The upper storey of the façade of the Khazneh, Petra, showing damage to the figures (Hornstein, 1895).

have revealed extensive forecourt structures, which suggest parallels with monumental tombs and palace architecture in places such as Nea Paphos in Cyprus, and at Alexandria in Egypt (Schmid 2001: 385-389).

The façade of the tomb is less weathered than many of the other monuments in Petra, and this is largely due to its relatively sheltered position at the end of the Siq, which protects it from the worst that nature can throw at the antiquities of Petra. However, the Khazneh has not entirely escaped the effects of time. The relief figures, which adorn the Khazneh, have unfortunately suffered severely at the hands of iconoclasts (see Fig. 196). The nineteenth century traveller would also have observed that one of the two disengaged columns flanking the entrance was missing. The broken pillar can be seen to the left of the picture in Fig 197, with the fallen part in front covered by sand and shrubs. The fallen portion of the pillar can be seen in Fig. 201. This pillar was restored in 1960 by the Department of Antiquities.

The height of the Khazneh presented the early travellers with a challenge when it came to making an accurate survey of the structure. It was dangerous and difficult to reach the upper storeys to record the architectural detail, and so much remained hidden. This situation changed in 1910. Before they embarked on their Transjordanian survey, Mackenzie and Newton met Gustav Dalman (director of the German Protestant Institute of Archaeology in Jerusalem) in Jerusalem, and learned that he was writing a study on the Khazneh for the PEF. The problems of accessibility to the obscure reaches of the monument were discussed, and so Mackenzie ordered a tall ladder in four parts to be made in Jerusalem especially, to enable the first accurate architectural drawings to be made, and academic study of the façade to be undertaken. This ladder was collected by Mackenzie and Newton at Ma'an, and from there transported to Petra, where, in November 1910, they met with Dalman and his local friend, Musa, who came from the village of Elgi nearby. The architect, Newton, was able to employ the ladder to gain access to these difficult reaches of the Khasneh, with

BEYOND THE RIVER

Fig. 197: An unusual view of the Khazneh at Petra taken by Francis Newton or Duncan Mackenzie in 1910 from a vantage point on the surrounding cliffs looking north-west.

the able assistance of Musa, who proved to be something of a mountain goat in this undertaking. The resulting drawings were the first truly accurate representations of the façade of the Khazneh that had been produced. Dalman was obviously rather pleased with the results that this collaborative effort achieved. On describing the events of the study, he wrote:

> ... when ... I saw Dr. Mackenzie's ladder standing at the 'Treasury' in its proper place, and my friend Musa on the rock at a tremendous height, to which few others had ventured to climb, dropping a long measuring-line from above the wonderful façade ... I knew victory was won and the Palestine Exploration Fund would have the honour of adding a new and important item to its unequalled reputation for the investigation of old and new Palestine. 1911:95-96)

Fig. 198: The view just inside the entrance of the Khazneh, Petra, looking right. The door leads to one of the side chambers of the tomb, whilst the steps lead to the central chamber. A third, unseen, chamber is to the left of the entrance (Hornstein 1895).

BEYOND THE RIVER

Fig. 199 (far right): *Musa of Elgi ascending the ladder to examine the façade.*

Fig. 200 (right): *Examining the façade of the Khazneh at Petra: raising the ladder.*

Fig. 201 (below): *Architect Francis Newton examining the architectural details of the door to the main chamber of the Khazneh (Mackenzie 1910). The broken pillar can be seen to the left of the picture, with the fallen part in front covered by sand and shrubs.*

The whole process was photographed by Mackenzie, and can be followed in these three photographs.

(PEF/P/MACK/59)

On the cliffs above and to the east of the Khazneh lies the High Place, or the Madhbah, in Arabic. This sacred area of the Nabataeans was photographed by Edward L. Wilson, an American editor and proprietor of the *Photographic Magazine*. He published the photograph in a volume entitled *Scripture Lands* in London in 1891. However, this discovery seems to have gone unnoticed until May 1900, when the site was visited by Professor G. L. Robinson of Chicago and the Reverend A. Forder of Jerusalem. They were quickly followed by Samuel Ives Curtiss, again accompanied by Forder, in the July of the same year. Curtiss published a detailed description of the High Place in the October issue of the *Quarterly Statement* (1900: 350-355). The sacred area

Fig. 202 (left): *Detail of a capital from the main lower order of the façade of the Khazneh (F.G. Newton 1910).*

Fig. 203 (below): *The High Place at Petra photographed by A.C. Dickie in 1907.*

Fig. 204: 'Zibb Attuf' ('Phallus of Mercy'), a monument near to the High Place at Petra photographed by Mackenzie or Newton in 1910.

comprises an altar and a sunken area, and various platforms and basins for sacrifice. The 'high place' or 'sacred mountain', is a common concept in many Semitic religions, including the Bronze and Iron Age Canaanite religion of the Levant, and indeed Judaism, which grew out of the same tradition. The pantheon of the Nabataeans shows strong links with the other religions of the area. The principal deity was the god Dushara, whose name means 'belonging to Shara', Edom's mountain range. This suggests that he was a local Edomite god, who was adapted by the Nabataeans once they settled in the area. Other major deities included the goddess Allat (or Al-Uzza), and Ba'al Shamin. Some members of the ruling dynasty also appear to have been deified after their death (as for example, the founder, Obodas I). These deities were often represented by stone carved rectangular stelae, sometimes with the addition of eyes (see Browning 1989: 45-49).

Near to the High Place is the monument known to the bedouins as 'Zibb Attuf', or the 'Phallus of Mercy'. These two obelisks stand seven metres tall, and were created by quarrying the mountain, which, apart from the obelisks themselves, was levelled in the process. The steps of the quarrying can be clearly seen in Mackenzie's photograph. The function and symbolism of the obelisks is not precisely known (perhaps they were just part of the quarrying process), but it is possible that the Arabic name preserves something of a phallic tradition of fertility worship. The site's proximity to the High Place could also indicate a religious function.

Back down in the Wadi Musa, and past the Khazneh, is Petra's Theatre, which for many years was thought to date to the Roman period after AD 106. Other scholars, however, believe it to date to between 4 BC and AD 27, during the reign of Aretas IV, when links with Rome were strong. Its 33 rows of seats, carved out of the rock, seated between 7,000 and 10,000 people, enough for the inhabitants of Petra, and its many visitors. The Theatre was photographed by John Shaw Smith in March 1852 as one of a series representing the first known true photographs of Petra. It was subsequently photographed by Hornstein in 1895 who took in a wider view giving a real context to the monument.

THE SOUTH

Fig. 205 (above): *The Theatre at Petra photographed by Smith in 1852.*

Fig. 206 (left): *Taken by Hornstein in 1895, this view shows the whole area surrounding the Theatre at Petra.*

Not far away, to the northeast of the Theatre, are the so-called Royal Tombs, cut into the mountain known as Jebel el-Kubtha. The first of these is the Urn Tomb, believed in local tradition to have been the law-courts, (el-Mahkamah), with the prison in the lower part of the monument.

Fig. 207: The Urn Tomb at Petra photographed for the first time in 1852 by John Shaw Smith.

Until very recently, this and other rock-carved tombs, were used by the local bedouins as shelter both for themselves and for their animals. The crude stone enclosures seen in some of the early photographs are evidence of this usage at the beginning of the twentieth century (see Fig. 208).

THE SOUTH

Fig. 208: The Urn Tomb at Petra. This photograph by Mackenzie or Newton (1910) is a rare view of the interior of the tomb at this date.

Fig. 209 (below left) *and Fig. 210* (below right) : *Forecourt colonnade and lower façade of the Urn Tomb at Petra photographed by Mackenzie or Newton in 1910.*

Fig. 211 (left): *A view of the Urn Tomb at Petra by Hornstein (1895), showing the monument in its wider setting. The much smaller Silk Tomb and the elaborate Corinthian Tomb are visible beyond.*

Next in the succession of Royal Tombs is the Palace Tomb. It has been suggested that this grandiose monument was modelled on Roman palaces of the day, possibly even Nero's Golden House (Browning 1989: 222-223).

Fig. 212: The Palace Tomb at Petra photographed by John Shaw Smith in 1852.

Fig. 213 (below): This photograph of Petra by John Shaw Smith, gives the view looking back along the Royal Tombs to the Urn Tomb, and shows both the Palace and Corinthian Tombs.

In the same area is the Tomb of Sextius Florentinus, the Governor of the Province of Arabia, who died in office in 129 AD, and was buried in Petra at his own wish. The tomb is the only one in Petra bearing an inscription (in Latin) with its date, and the name of the son who constructed it. The inscription read:

To Lucius Ninius, son of Lucius Papirius Sextius Florentinus, Triumvir for coining gold and silver, Military Tribune of Legion I Minerva, Quaestor of the province of Achaia, Tribune of the Plebs, Legate of Legion VIIII Hispania, Proconsul of the province of Narbonensis, Legate of Augustus, Propraetor of the Province of Arabia, most dutiful father, in accordance with his own will.

The Tomb of Sextius Florentinius was captured very dramatically in a photograph by Hornstein in 1895 (Fig. 214). The remarkable swirling patterns of the rock itself, for which Petra is rightly so famous, are especially dramatic. One can also see how the erosion has eaten into the detail of the façade, so that it appears, somewhat perversely, that a beautiful building is slowly emerging from the rock, rather than being erased by time.

Fig. 214: The Tomb of Sextius Florentius at Petra photographed by Hornstein in 1895.

Continuing down the side of the Wadi Musa is the main colonnaded street of Petra. At the end of the colonnaded street, between the nymphaeum and the Qasr el-Bint, one comes to the triumphal arch or Temenos Gate, which once formed the entrance to the Temenos itself, the large open area in front of the Qasr el-Bint, one of the main temples in Petra.

Fig. 215: A view by Hornstein showing the ruins of the Temenos Gate at Petra as they appeared in 1895, with the Qasr el-Bint and rugged mountains behind.

The Qasr el-Bint (the Palace of the Girl) is also known as Qasr Faroun (the Palace of Pharoah), or Qasr Bint Faroun (the Palace of the Daughter of the Pharoah). Although a Nabataean temple, probably built during the reign

Fig. 216: The Qasr el-Bint, photographed by Hornstein in 1895.

of Obodas II (30-9 BC), its attribution to the Pharoahs is indicative of the legendary status of the Egyptian monarchs in local Arab tradition. As with the Khazneh (also known as the Khazneh Faroun), they were the only people seen as having been capable of constructing such grand monuments. The Qasr el-Bint was photographed by Hornstein in 1895, but since then a great

deal of excavation and reconstruction has taken place, which has totally changed the appearance and setting of the building.

About two kilometres to the north-east of the Tememos Arch, one arrives at the site called Mughur en-Nasara (the Caves of the Christians), also known as Khirbet en-Nasara (the Ruins of the Christians). Unlike the classical façades of the Royal Tombs and the Khazneh, the tombs in this area combine much more obviously the architectural traditions of east and west. The entrances to the tombs are given a classical style porch, whilst the 'upper storey' is decorated with a typical oriental 'crow's step' motif. This stepped design had its origins in the Assyrian empire of the eighth century BC

Fig. 217 (above): *Petra: two tombs at Mughur en-Nasara looking north-east, photographed by Mackenzie or Newton in 1910. On both tombs, an Egyptian style cavetto cornice can clearly be seen between the classical 'lower storey' and the Assyrian-style 'upper storey'.*

Fig. 218 (left): *A tomb on the north-east wall of the Mughur en-Nasara at Petra, photographed by Mackenzie or Newton in 1910. This tomb has a much more purely classical façade, with an archived pediment over the doorway. Although fairly simple in its detail, it is finely proportioned and undoubtedly would have been the tomb of a person of some importance.*

A monument of special fame in Petra, second perhaps only to the Khazneh, is the Deir (the Monastery). This enormous sepulchral monument lies around 1,500 metres to the north of Kasr Bint Faroun, high up in the surrounding hills. Probably carved late in the first century AD (Schmid 2001: 397-398), it is one of the largest monuments in Petra, measuring 50 metres wide and nearly 45 metres high to the top of the urn. Its door is 8 metres high (Harding 1959:

Fig. 219 (right): *The Deir at Petra. The rather grainy image on the right is remarkable for its early date; it was taken by John Shaw Smith in 1852.*

Fig. 220 (below): *The same view was hotographed by Hornstein in 1895.*

135). The Deir shares many similar features with the Khazneh and the Corinthian Tomb, but unlike both of these, the architectural decorations are stark and simple, lending it a sense of massive monumentality.

The views from the Deir are truly spectacular. The rugged contours of the Edomite range, and the striking contrast between the colour of the rock and the clear blue of the desert sky make for one of the most memorable landscapes in Transjordan. Looking west from the Deir, one can see right across the Wadi Arabah to Palestine and Sinai. At a distance to the south of it, one can see Jebel Harun (Mount Hor) with the old shrine of Aaron's Tomb at its summit.

Reaching Mount Hor and Aaron's Tomb was not always easy. Local traditions concerning the sanctity of the spot, coupled with the bandits that sometimes preyed on unwary travellers, meant that outsiders were not always given access. In 1812, Burckhardt found that despite his disguise as an Arab, the local guide would not take him to the tomb itself. The pioneering traveller had to satisfy himself with sacrificing a goat on the slopes of Mount Hor, and even this made his guide uneasy:

> While I was in the act of slaying the animal, my guide exclaimed aloud, "O Haroun look upon us. O Haroun protect us and forgive us! Oh Haroun be content with our good intentions, for it is but a lean goat!..." We then dressed the best part of the flesh for our supper, as expeditiously as possible, for the guide was afraid of the fire being seen, and of its attracting hither some robbers" (1822: 431).

Fig. 221: A view of Mount Hor from the Deir, Petra, taken by Frank Mason Good in 1866-7.

BEYOND THE RIVER

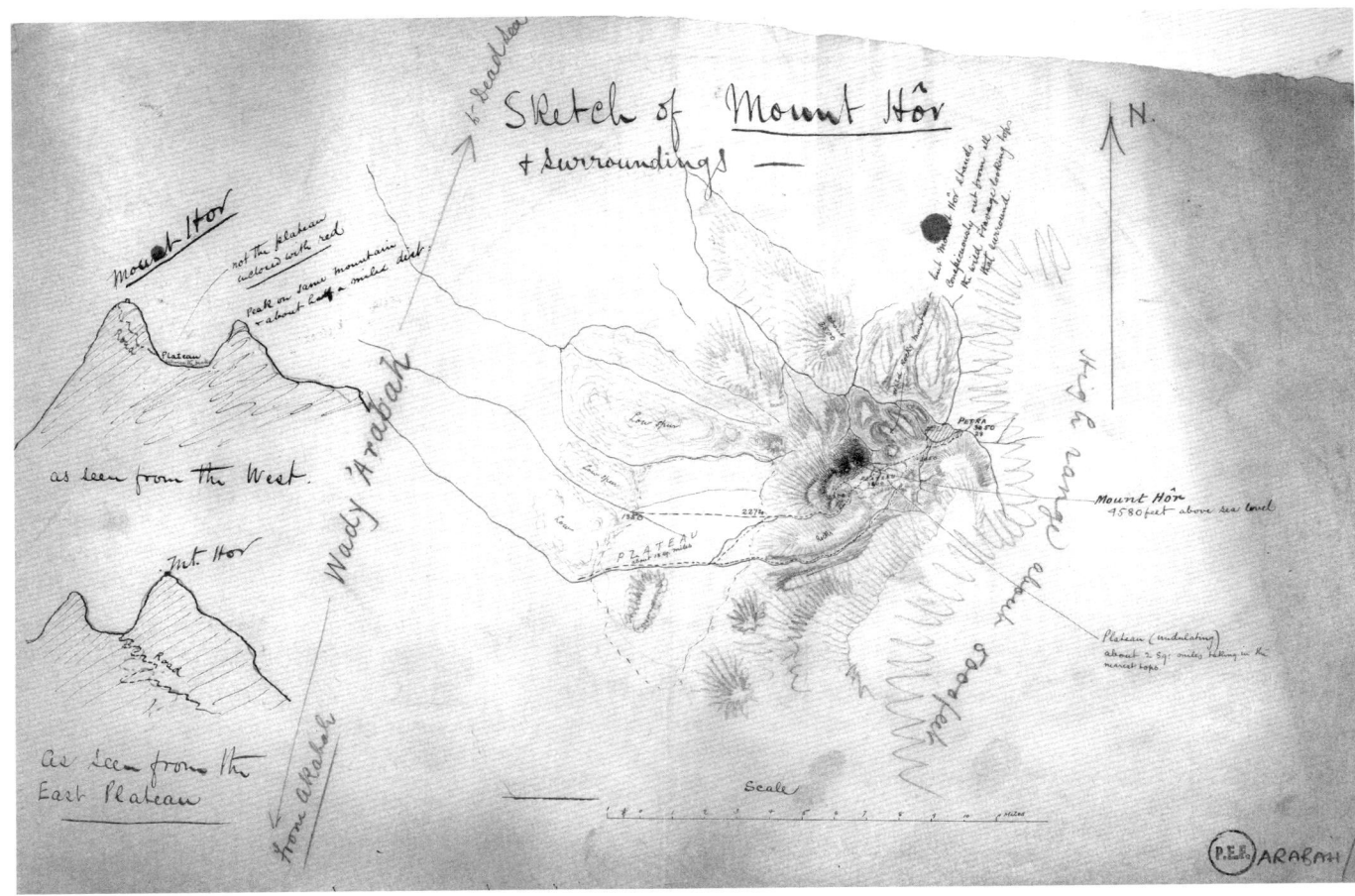

Fig. 222: This sketch map of Petra and Mount Hor was drawn by Mr Armstrong and Captain Kitchener in 1883-4 during the Wadi Arabah Survey.

Fig. 223 (right): View of Mount Hor, with Aaron's Tomb on the summit, taken by Hornstein during his attempted visit in 1895.

THE SOUTH

Hornstein, visiting in 1895, also encountered problems trying to visit the mountain and the tomb of its resident saint:

> After dinner we rested a while, and then told the sheikhs that we would like to go to Jebel Haroon, Mount Hor. They refused to listen to such a thing, for they said if they took us up some evil would assuredly befall them before the year was out ... Seeing we were determined, they tried to dissuade us by saying it was too late, and we should not get back till late at night. However, we told them we would try, so, starting up a very rough and rocky path, we reached the top of the wadi. From there we had a magnificent view of the mountain, which still seemed a long way off. The Arabs had said the truth when they told us we should not get back till night. The sun was already near the horizon, and would have set by the time we reached the top, so that it would have been impossible to take any photo, as I had hoped to ... we decided that the only thing to be done was to get as near as possible and take a photo. On the north-east peak is situated the tomb of Aaron. We could see the white dome and little square building enclosing the tomb. It was a great disappointment not to be able to ascend. (1898: 101-102).

To judge from his photographs Hornstein, was more fortunate on a second trip to Petra that he made with Sir Charles Wilson of the PEF in 1899. On this occasion he was clearly able to enter the tomb itself. Believed to be the resting place of prophet Haroun (Aaron), the brother of prophet Musa

Fig. 224: A closer view of the exterior of Aaron's Tomb on Mount Hor taken by Hornstein during a second visit to Petra in 1899.

Fig. 225: Aaron's Tomb on Mount Hor, showing the interior of the tomb, with the sarcophagus draped in a funerary robe. Photographed by Hornstein in 1899.

Fig. 226: (right): View from Mount Hor looking down into the Wadi Arabah, taken by Hornstein in 1899.

(Moses), the shrine has been, for many centuries, a mosque. An Arabic inscription over the door declares the building to have been erected by Muhammad, son of Qaloun, Sultan of Egypt, in the year 739 Hejira (AD 1338), at the command of his father. It was further restored round AH 900 (about AD 1495) (Taylor 1993: 76-79).

Looking south and west from Mount Hor, one can see down into the Wadi Arabah and across to the mountains of Sinai. An evocative photograph taken by Hornstein, probably in 1899, shows this view from the fortress-mountains of Edom down to the ancient caravan trails that were the life-blood of the Nabataean kingdom, and the gateways to distant lands beyond Transjordan.

NOTES

1. The Nabataeans are not distinct in the archaeological evidence from Jordan until about 100 BC, despite the references to them being in the area in the historical texts. It may be that they remained a primarily nomadic (and archaeologically less visible) society until this time, when the decline of the Seleucid dynasty, and the discovery of the direct sea route from South Arabia to India, made a settled lifestyle, as a means of controlling the trade, more feasible. In addition, the possibilities for settled agriculture in the region of Petra and Transjordan may have been more numerous than in their homelands. There are two current theories concerning their origins. The first argues for a north-eastern Arabian, Mesopotamian, or even Iranian origin, based on the similarities in pottery style, and perhaps more importantly, possible similarities in dialect and language structure. (See Schmid 2001: 367-370). The second argument looks to the Hejaz region and north-western Arabia as a more likely point of origin, by virtue of the fact that alternative theories can be shown to be unconvincing, and that the concentration of Nabataean sites in this region would suggest a likely homeland. (See Parr 2003: 29 – 32)

2. In 1995, the Petra National Trust, (a Society founded in 1989 under the patronage of H.M. Queen Nour Al-Hussein) was presented with financial assistance by the Swiss Government to execute this important project, in memory of the famous Swiss explorer, John Lewis Burckhardt. The Nabataeans constructed a water channel running along the whole length of the Siq, which formed a part of their elaborate water system. Other remains include 'betyls', or holy standing stones, and numerous shrines and niches to the Nabataean deities.

— Chapter Nine —

The Arab Revolt:
A New Era

Detail of the photograph by A. Reid documenting the arrival in Cairo of Sherif Abdullah early in 1914. (See pages 212-3 for full picture.)

In late 1913 and early 1914, a survey of the Negev desert was conducted under the auspices of the PEF. This survey, now known as the 'Wilderness of Zin Survey', extended as far south as the Sinai and the border with Egypt, into the Wadi Arabah, and as far east as Petra. Its purpose was to map a region that had not yet been covered by the previous PEF surveys.

The motivations for the survey, as explained to the Turkish officials, when the PEF applied for permission to conduct the work, were entirely academic and scholarly. Given the PEF's previous record of surveying in the area, it seems that, on the verge of war with Britain, the Turkish administration were eventually satisfied with this explanation, and allowed the expedition to take place. But that was only half the story.

On 21 October 1913, Colonel W. Coote Hedley of the War Office was elected to the Committee of the PEF. The PEF had always had connections with the army, particularly with the Royal Engineers[1], but Hedley's position within the Geographical Section of the War Office was significant. This section was concerned with gathering geographical information that could be used in the now almost inevitable war against Germany, and also against the Ottoman Empire. Prior to his appointment, the PEF had received confidential correspondence from the government on the desirability of a survey in this specific area, for the purposes of the effective defence of the Egyptian Frontier in the event of war[2].

It is certain that Kitchener, now Lord Kitchener of Kartoum, was interested in this survey, and was instrumental in bringing it about. This was hardly surprising, given his previous involvement with the PEF in both the Survey of Western Palestine in the 1870's and in the Wadi Arabah Survey of 1883-4. With his close association with the study of the region, he knew exactly which areas were not already mapped adequately.

The PEF acquired the services of Captain S. F. Newcombe R.E. to conduct the 'geographical' (or military) survey, and so began looking for an archaeologist to direct the academic work. Their first choice, the Egyptologist T. E. Peet, was unavailable, and so they looked further afield. Sir Frederick Kenyon, Director of the British Museum, suggested two young archaeologists who were then employed at the Museum's excavations at Carchemish on the Euphrates, a site far away from the southern Levant, in what is now the no-man's land between Syria and Turkey. The men were Leonard Woolley, who would become one of Britain's most eminent archaeologists, and T.E. Lawrence who was destined for fame as Lawrence of Arabia, hero of the Arab Revolt.

Whilst it is true that both men would become involved in subsequent military and intelligence operations during the Great War, there is no evidence to support the theory that the two scholars were made privy to the military nature of the operation prior to their arrival in the Negev. Their role was to act as archaeological cover rather than to engage in any active espionage or other operation. If anything, the significance for the later career of Lawrence in particular was that it was here, in the barren region of the Negev and Wadi Arabah, amongst the bedouin tribes, that he learnt the 'desert craft' that would stand him in good stead in the years to come.

THE ARAB REVOLT

A month into the survey, the group split into two teams so as to cover the ground more effectively. Woolley stayed in the Negev with Yusuf Canaan, a Palestinian who had worked on several PEF projects as an excavation foreman and compiler of folk histories. Lawrence and Newcombe went south and east, to the Wadi Arabah and Transjordan. Upon reaching Aqaba, the survey ground to a halt, as the local Turkish Governor had no knowledge of the survey, and therefore refused permission for work to continue. Whilst Newcombe was inclined not to aggravate the situation, and had received instructions from Kitchener to refrain from surveying any areas for which permission had not been granted, Lawrence was much more determined to carry on regardless. This brought him into direct conflict with the Turkish authorities, and after an illicit trip to Geziret Faroun (the 'Island of the Pharaoh') he was escorted out of the area by the police. He managed to give his guard the slip at Petra, before continuing up to Damascus, and then to Aleppo on the Hejaz railway, where he joined up once more with Woolley. This incident was reported to the PEF by Woolley:

> Mr Lawrence was forbidden to visit Geziret Faroun (he had to swim out to it on a water can) and to make any plans or photographs. The [Turkish] Government refused also to give him a telegram sent by the British consul at Damascus, and sent soldiers with him to stop him going up Mt. Hor:- it was only by tiring out their camels that he was able to shake them off and climb the mountain.[3]

Fig. 227: An interesting photograph taken by Lawrence in 1914 of Geziret Faroun. It shows the island, with its castle, taken at fairly close range, obviously during Lawrence's secret trip to the island. Although it is geographically part of Egypt, as it stands a short distance from the Egyptian point of Taba, Geziret Faroun is an important part of the Gulf of Aqaba that is now shared between four powers: Egypt, Israel, Jordan, and Saudi Arabia. Given the present difficulties in the region, it is surprising that the area has become so important both for commercial shipping and tourism.

The two archaeologists returned to England in June 1914, and by the autumn, both men had assumed positions within the army, Woolley as an officer in the Royal Field Artillery, and Lawrence within the War Office. The significance of the military survey conducted by Newcombe was considerable. Without the detailed knowledge of the terrain and water resources that it provided, it would have been impossible for General Allenby to conduct the hugely successful Beersheba Campaign of 1917 that marked the beginning of the end of the war in the East.

Kitchener wanted the archaeological report to be published as soon as possible, but due to the constraints of Woolley's time at the army barracks, this task fell primarily to Lawrence. He delivered the manuscript to the PEF on 3 December 1914, and at that point, the formal association between the PEF and Woolley and Lawrence came to an end. Newcombe, however, was to remain a loyal supporter of the PEF, and after the war, was a member of the Executive Committee for a number of years[4].

The roots of the Arab Revolt – the uprising of the Arab Tribes against Ottoman rule – can be traced back to the Napoleonic era and the French occupation of Egypt from 1799 to 1802. Although short, the occupation opened the door to serious changes in Egypt's government. With the French withdrawal, the Egyptian government was no longer functional. In 1805, Muhammad Ali Pasha (an Albanian officer, who was sent with an Albanian contingent by the Sultan of Turkey to fight against Bonaparte), was appointed *Wali* (or Governor), and thereby took control of Egypt. After consolidating his power through the eradication of the Mamluks, he assisted the Turks in their wars in the Arabian Peninsula, the Sudan, and Greece (including Crete). In 1831 he started a campaign of his own in Syria. It was his son Ibrahim Pasha, however, who finally conquered the area, and ruled it for ten years, during which time he introduced a number of cultural and economic developments. During the course of the nineteenth century, as American and European missionaries and travellers began to visit the Levant in greater numbers, the educational standards of the region began to evolve. This greater knowledge fuelled a feeling of general dissatisfaction amongst the population with what was increasingly seen as an out-dated Ottoman administration.

The situation was further aggravated by the estrangement that developed between the new rulers of Turkey in 1908, after the revolution of the Committee of Union and Progress succeeded in limiting the powers of Sultan Abdul Hamid, and took over complete control of the Government. Arabs were no longer able to convince themselves that these 'Young Turks', with their pan-Turkmanic aspirations, and extreme nationalistic Turkish feelings, were their brothers under the umbrella of the common faith of Islam.

This complicated situation was being watched carefully by Sherif Hussein Bin Ali of Mecca and his four sons Ali, Abdullah, Feisal and Zaid. As the descendants of prophet Mohammed, these Hashemite princes felt a strong sense of duty to the holy places of Islam and the Arab lands as a whole. Their ambition extended beyond their role as the religious Sherifs of Mecca. Their political thinking was, no doubt, influenced by the Arab secret organizations that had meanwhile become active in Syria, fostering Arab nationalism. The movement for Arab Reform acquired momentum when a joint committee of 86 members was founded, comprising Syrian and Egyptian Arab nationalists. They held a six-day conference in Paris in June 1913 to discuss the issues at stake. They made a point of stressing that they desired to maintain the unity of the Ottoman Empire and were only demanding the recognition of Arab rights as partners in the state. Nevertheless the Turks, whose party secretary attended the conference, were not happy with the developments, and their position continued to be antagonistic.

During 1914, Sherif Hussein's second son, Prince Abdullah, was a delegate in the Turkish Parliament in Istanbul, and was therefore aware of the wave of antagonism against Arab aspirations. He was also suspicious that the Turks were scheming to depose his father, Sherif Hussein Bin Ali of Mecca. He made his feelings known to Ronald Storrs, the Oriental Secretary of the British Residency in Cairo, and in April 1914, whilst a guest of the Khedive (Ottoman governor), paid a visit to Lord Kitchener, the British Agent in Egypt. Storrs acted as translator at this meeting. What Abdullah actually said to Kitchener is not entirely clear, but it appears that he was seeking British support for an Arab uprising against Ottoman rule (Fromkin 1991: 98-99).

These contacts were the precursors of more concentrated negotiations, when Kitchener became Secretary of State for War in London, and the correspondence started between Sherif Hussein and Sir Henry MacMahon, the new British representative in Egypt. The scene was truly set for the Arab Revolt when the British, through a note dated the 30 August 1915, sent by MacMahon to Sherif Hussein, confirmed Kitchener's and Britain's support and approval for the Arab cause for independence, and for the establishment of a future Arab Caliphate (Antonius 1938: 416).

On 9 June 1916 Hussein Bin Ali, Sherif of Mecca, declared the Arab Revolt against the Turkish Administration in the Arabian Peninsula. T. E. Lawrence was sent with Ronald Storrs, and arrived in Jeddah in mid-October the same year. During his few days' stay in Jeddah, Lawrence struck up a friendly relationship with Sherif Abdullah, the future Emir of the Hashemite Emirate of Jordan, of whom he wrote later:

> Abdullah, on a white mare, came to us softly, with a bevy of richly armed slaves on foot about him, through silent respectful salutes of the town. He was flushed with his success at Taif and happy. I was seeing him for the first time while Storrs was an old friend and on the best of terms; yet before long, as they spoke together, I began to suspect him of a constant cheerfulness. His eyes had a continued twinkle; and though only thirty-five he was putting on flesh. It might be due to much laughter. He jested with all comers in most easy fashion: Yet when we fell into serious talk, the veil of humour seemed to fade away, as he chose his words and argued shrewdly. Of course, he was in discussion with Storrs, who demanded a high standard from his opponent. (1927: 13)

Fig. 228: (following pages): Photograph by A. Reid documenting the arrival in Cairo of Sherif Abdullah early in 1914. The prince is seated in a Rolls Royce in front of the main entrance of the Rifai Mosque (Madani 1979: 90). The picture shows a few of the prince's entourage in the crowd, two civilian officials seated next to the prince, one wearing an ordinary trilby hat while the second has a dress top hat. At least 12 British officers appear, together with an Egyptian high-ranking officer, seated opposite the prince, probably his ADC. As the Khedive's distinguished guest, Ronald Storrs is seated next to the driver, giving him instructions. In addition to a good number of officials and civilian dignitaries, there are at least six turbaned 'Ulema (Muslim scholars), and three local Egyptian dignitaries. On the left side, next to a solitary police sergeant, one of the Emir's bodyguard slaves appears with his dagger, and a stick in his left hand. Another stick appears in the left hand of a Hejazi person who most probably was a member of the prince's entourage.

Lawrence did not stay long in Jeddah, and after a few days he was on his way to meet Sherif Ali at Rabegh, north of Jeddah, who had his father's orders to transfer him to Sherif Feisal's camp at Wadi Safra, commanding the military operation against the Turkish garrison in Medina. It was then that he felt, at first glance, that Feisal was the man he had come to Arabia to seek – the leader who would bring the Arab revolt to full glory (Lawrence 1935: 91).

The Red Sea port of Aqaba was of great importance to the Arab Revolt. With it, the Arabs could secure their supply lines, but it was strongly held by a Turkish force. Sherif Nasir, Auda Abu Tayih, and Lawrence organized the campaign with growing numbers of Arab volunteers from many tribes. They forced the Turkish garrison at Kethira to surrender, and the posts below it to be evacuated. The port of Aqaba itself is surrounded on all sides by natural barriers – mountains with narrow passes. Given this setting, the Turks were convinced that any attack would come from the sea: they never expected to be attacked by land from the north. The unexpected attack on the Aqaba garrison was successful and the Arab Revolt accomplished the occupation of the town on 6 July 1917.

In the First World War, there were two major theatres of Allied operations in the Levant; the western in the area of the Suez Canal and Palestine, under

Fig. 229: Photograph taken by T. E. Lawrence during the Wilderness of Zin Survey in 1914. It shows the Nagab el-Aqaba, the narrow pass through which one could access the port of Aqaba from Sinai and the west.

THE ARAB REVOLT

Fig. 230 (above): *A photograph taken by Hull in 1883 showing a date palm grove near to Aqaba. Date plantations were, and continue to be, a useful, sustainable source of income in this once remote district.*

Fig. 231 (left): *A view taken by Hull in 1883 showing the head of the Gulf of Aqaba looking southwest towards Sinai and Egypt.*

Fig. 232: View of the walled town of Aqaba with the mountains of Transjordan behind (Hull 1883). Outside the walls, to the left of the photograph, is an encampment of Muslim pilgrims on their return from Mecca, on their way to their homes in the southern parts of Palestine, Sinai, Egypt, and the North African states further on.

Fig. 233 (right): A photograph by Rhodes showing the Damieh area, still famous for its bridge that connects the Nablus-Palestinian side with the Balqa-Jordanian side. It shows quite a volume of water in the river bed and a thick forest of trees in the Zor area on the banks. In the background is a meandering dotted line of Allied cavalry making its way down from the barren mountains of the West Bank to the crossing.

General Allenby (the Beersheba Campaign), and the Arab Revolt in the east, coming up from Medina, under the command of Abdullah, Feisal, and Lawrence, with a thrust for Aqaba and the Transjordanian plateau. The main focus of the joint campaign was Damascus, and northwards to the Turkish border. Documenting the campaign are a number of fascinating images, all taken in 1917 and 1918 by Captain Arthur Rhodes, a young New Zealander serving in the ANZAC divisions. They record the activity of the Allied troops in the Jordan valley during the crossing of the river Jordan to join the forces of the Arab Revolt, and the operations thereafter.

From its beginnings in Mecca in 1916, the Arab Revolt spread all over the regions of the Hijaz and greater Syria. It culminated in the Declaration of Arab Independence and the proclamation of Prince Faisal as king of Syria, and his father Sherif Hussein Bin Ali as king of the Hijaz.

THE ARAB REVOLT

Fig. 234 (left): A view of the cavalry negotiating their way across the Wadi Nuweimeh, a tributary of the Jordan, before making the crossing into Transjordan at the Ghoraniyeh Ford, now the location of the Allenby Bridge. The picture by Rhodes conveys how crossing even a small river such as the Nuweimeh could become a time-consuming business for a cavalry detachment .

Fig. 235 (left): This photograph by Rhodes shows a parade of the Canterbury Mounted Rifles in the Jordan Valley in 1917, before the push northwards to chase the retreating Turkish forces under the command of the German General Liman von Sanders.

Fig. 236 (left): Taken in the Jordan Valley, looking towards the Mount of Beatitudes behind Jericho, this photograph by Rhodes shows captured Turkish troops and cattle on the move. The abundant flowers, which are providing at least the cattle with a feast, would indicate that this photograph was taken in early Spring, 1918.

BEYOND THE RIVER

Fig. 237 (above): *The ingenious engineering solutions of the Allied forces were one of the key factors in their eventual victory over the Turks. The 'Londoner's Bridge' (named after the regiment which built it) provided a safe crossing over the River Jordan, east of Jericho, close to an old, but unusable bridge, which can just be seen in the background of this Rhodes image. The waters of the river are swollen with winter or spring rain, which can be torrential even this far to the south.*

Fig. 238 (below): *A photograph by Rhodes showing the grim reality of war, with dead Turkish troops lined up ready for burial in the Jordan Valley. The troops of the ANZAC divisions view the scene.*

THE ARAB REVOLT

Fig. 240 (below): *A photograph by Rhodes showing a group of Arab fighting men on the move in the Moab hills. One western Allied soldier is just visible, towards the back of the caravan, in his distinctive trousers, jacket and hat.*

Fig. 239 (above): *This photograph by Rhodes shows an Australian soldier, in the area north of Jericho, with a group of four armed men of the Arab Revolt. Two young women look on.*

Fig. 241 (above): *ANZAC soldiers riding near Amman, with a group of Turkish officer POWs, who, unlike their regular troops, were granted the privilege of a mount for their journey into captivity (Photograph taken by Rhodes).*

Fig. 242 (opposite): *A remarkable photograph taken by A. Reid in Jerusalem in 1921. It shows three of Sherif Abdullah's entourage. In November 1990, Sheikh Jwayber el-'Otaiby, a Jordanian dignitary, then aged 95, who had accompanied Abdullah to Amman and Jerusalem, recognized the three and named them as Salim Ibn Jaber, an attendant of Sherif Shaker bin Zain in the middle, with Ahmad Wasfi, attendant to Sherif Abdullah, on his right, and Salih (Sheikh Jwayber could not remember his second name), an attendant of Abdullah, on his left.*

With the end of the Great War in October 1918, came a new era for the Middle East. Following the defeat of the Ottoman Empire, the region's future was uncertain, with tensions between the Great Powers (particularly France and Britain) and the local leaders coming to a head. Sherif Feisal, Lawrence's great hope for the Arabs, briefly controlled Damascus, only to be ousted by the French. The result was French Mandate rule in what is now Syria. Transjordan itself was subjected to a variety of administrative experiments, including the formation in 1920 of local (but with British advisers attached) governments in Kerak, Ajlun and Balqa. The famous peace conference in Cairo, in the spring of 1921 attempted to resolve some of the outstanding issues of the day. Proceedings were interrupted when Sherif Abdullah, the elder brother of Feisal, based in Ma'an, announced himself as Vice-King of Syria in support of his brother Feisal. A few days later, he journeyed by train to Amman, accompanied by a *katiba*, a battalion of Hashemite soldiers and a guard of Hashemite tribal retainers, to rally bedouin support for his move to drive the French out of Damascus and bring the entire region under Hashemite rule. Sir Herbert Samuel, the first Governor of the British Mandate Government of Palestine invited Abdullah to Jerusalem for negotiations. The meeting between Abdullah and Auni Abd el-Hadi representing the Arabs, and Herbert Samuel, Winston Churchill and T.E. Lawrence, the last two fresh from Cairo, took place on 19 March. The outcome of this meeting was the foundation of the new Hashemite Emirate of Jordan, with Abdullah, the second son of Hussein of Mecca, as its Emir (El-Edroos 1980: 206-207).

And so our tour of old Transjordan draws to its close. With the establishment of the Hashemite Emirate in Transjordan, the region began to develop, at a startling rate, into the populous and modern country that we are familiar with today. This marked the end of an old way of life for many, together with the landscapes and vistas that their traditions produced. Mud brick and stone dwellings have gradually been replaced by concrete built houses and apartments, although the bedouins still retain their tents in some cases. Agricultural machinery and modern farming technologies have transformed the economy and the countryside. Industry and commerce have drawn huge numbers of people to the rapidly growing cities and tourist attractions. The frontier territory, revealed in these photographs of the nineteenth and early twentieth centuries, stands in stark contrast to the sophisticated modern country, and one to which we can only return through these images, and the traveller's tales they illustrate.

Fig. 243: In the photograph (opposite) by A. Reid, taken in Jerusalem in 1921, Sherif Abdullah stands with Sheikh Jwayber el-'Otaiby on his right, and Mohammad el-'Asbali on his left. Both of them came with Sherif Abdullah to Transjordan in 1921. The first is a member of the Otaibeh Tribal Federation while the second is a member of the Ashraf of Taif.

NOTES

1. The relationship between the PEF and Her Majesty's Government was complex, but for the most part an informal one. With a slowly disintegrating Ottoman Empire, and a growing British presence in Egypt, government officials could certainly see the benefit of the survey work that the PEF was interested in carrying out in the potentially strategic area of the southern Levant. It was on this basis that the best officers in the Royal Engineers were repeatedly made available to the PEF. In this relationship, however, it was always the PEF who decided what

needed to be done, whilst the Government and army were very happy to benefit from the results. The Wilderness of Zin survey was the one time that a direct order to the PEF, when military details did not prevent them, was given from the army or the Government to conduct a survey. During and after the war, relations remained relatively close, but on a less direct basis. The PEF contributed copies of its maps to the War Office, free of charge, and there was always room on the PEF's Committee for a military man for many years to come.

2. Copy of letter (FO371/1812, fos.279) in the archives of the Palestine Exploration Fund (PEF/DA/ZIN 1), from the Directorate of Military Operations (M.O.4/Africa/341), to the Under Secretary of State for Foreign Affairs. The letter is dated 19 September 1913, and is marked 'Confidential'. The written note states, 'Submitted by Colonel Hedley to Committee of No. 4, 1913.'

3. PEF/DA/ZIN/55: Letter from Leonard Woolley in Aleppo to Sir Charles Watson of the PEF dated 7 March 1914.

4. A recent analysis by T. Sam N. Moorhead of the Wilderness of Zin survey, its implications for the subsequent progress of the war in the Middle East, and Lawrence's military career, can be found in the new edition of *The Wilderness of Zin* (Woolley and Lawrence 2003).

Appendix I

The Changing Face of Photography & Biographies of the Photographers

The Changing Face of Photography

The photographs in this volume range in date from 1852 to 1921, the formative years of both photography as a discipline, and of the region of Transjordan, as it grew from a neglected province of the Ottoman Empire into an independent Emirate.

The first photographic process was invented in 1835 by W.H. Talbot, when he discovered that ordinary paper treated with a salt solution and silver nitrate, and exposed to light, became darker. His results were published in 1839, opening the way for the development of a number of photographic methods. (Coe & Haworth-Booth 1983: 27). One of the most common of these early techniques was known as Calotype, in which treated paper was exposed directly to produce a negative image[1]. The photographs of John Shaw Smith are an example of this technique.

It was not long before pioneers of photography were taking the technology and using it in exotic Near Eastern locations, particularly Egypt, the Holy Land, and Turkey. With the invention of the Wet Collodion Process in 1851, which employed glass plates to carry the negative image,[2] many more enthusiasts began to practice the art of photography.

The photographic equipment of these early pioneers was both complex and cumbersome, as well as being extremely expensive. The glass plates that carried the negative images were fragile and very heavy, as were the cameras and bottles of chemicals. Many glass plates broke before a positive could be printed, or the extreme climatic conditions of heat and cold caused the emulsions to start to separate from the glass. Exposure times were very long, sometimes requiring human subjects to stand stock still for several minutes or risk a ghostly, and sometimes atmospheric, blurring effect. Given these technical problems, it is quite extraordinary that so many superb photographs of such a remote country have survived. As time passed, photographic technology became more portable, more 'user friendly', and slightly less prohibitively expensive. The introduction of the Gelatine Dry Plate method during the 1880s had a significant impact.[3] By the end of the 1900s more and more people were able to take photographs of their journeys. This phenomenon had two noticeable effects.

Firstly, there was an occasional but inevitable lowering of the technical quality of some of the photographs. With more 'amateurs' taking their own shots, there were increasingly cases of fascinating subjects being rather poorly served by the shaky hand on the other side of the lens. Be this as it may, the photographs serve as a unique record of an extraordinary time and place.

Secondly, the character and subject of the images also changed from earlier times. Instead of the large format landscape and architectural photographs of the earlier expeditions, the people of the country began to make more of an entrance. With smaller, more manageable equipment, shots were often less formal, more immediate in their feel, and could therefore reveal the realities of life that the earlier photographs were unable to show.

It is said that the camera never lies. Even before the digital age this statement was not entirely accurate. The photographer chooses what subject is to be photographed, and how that subject is to be treated. In this sense, as a document of a time and a place, photographs should be approached as one would approach any historical document; that is with an intelligent and critical eye. The photographs in this volume document the subtle changes in the interests and motivation of the photographers and travellers, and in doing so reveal a dual view of the untamed country beyond the river; as it appeared to the Western world, and, perhaps, a little of how it truly was.

The Photographers

BLISS, Frederick Jones (1859-1937)

Born in Lebanon in 1859, the archaeologist Dr Frederick Jones Bliss was an American national, and son of Daniel Bliss, the founder of the American University of Beirut. Although he suffered throughout his life from ill health, he undertook a significant amount of research in the Levant. His training as a field archaeologist began in Egypt with Sir William Matthew Flinders Petrie. Petrie was himself a pioneer of stereoscopic photography, and so perhaps it is no surprise that Bliss was very comfortable with a camera. He first worked for the Palestine Exploration Fund in 1890, when he was employed as assistant to Petrie on the Fund's excavations at Tell el-Hesi in southern Palestine. He continued as the excavation's Director until 1893, and subsequently at a number of other PEF excavations in Palestine, including Jerusalem (where he was assisted by Archibald C. Dickie), and the Shephela sites of Tell Zakariya, Tell es-Safi, Tell Judeideh, and Tell Sandahannah. At the end of the nineteenth century, Bliss was instrumental in assisting the Ottoman government in establishing an archaeological museum in Jerusalem, a development that did not receive the full support of the PEF in London.[4] During the First World War, he served as advisor on the antiquities of Syria and Palestine to General Allenby. (Blakely 1997: 332-333). Bliss's photographs of his excavations are particularly scientific and informative by the standards of the day, and his images from his 1895 trip to Transjordan show the same attention to detail, in focusing on the archaeological and architectural subjects.

BONFILS FAMILY (1867-1916)

The Bonfils family was one of the most successful and prolific photographic studios operating in Palestine in the nineteenth century. The French photographer Felix Bonfils (1931-85) settled in Beirut in 1867 and established the family business there with his wife Marie-Lydie. His son, Adrien, became active in the firm in the later decades of the nineteenth century. After her husband's death in 1885, Marie-Lydie continued to run the business until 1916. The Bonfils family concentrated on producing photographs of locations throughout the eastern Mediterranean for the tourist market, and most of their photographs of the Southern Levant concentrate on Western Palestine, particularly Jerusalem, although some photographs of Transjordanian sites were produced (Perez 1988:141). Those in this volume are from the northern shores of the Dead Sea.

DICKIE, Archibald Campbell,(1868-1941)

The architect, Archibald C. Dickie, was first employed by the PEF as assistant to Dr Bliss in Jerusalem from March 1895 until June 1897[5]. Following this, he practis ed as an architect in London until 1912, and was Master of Design at the Architectural Association School, also in London. He became a member of the PEF's Executive Committee in 1906, and served as Assistant Secretary at their offices in London from 1910 until 1912. At this time, he was appointed Professor of Architecture at Manchester University, a post he held for 21 years. He was Professor Emeritus from 1933 until his death in 1941 (Blythe(?) 1942:5-7).

In the winter of 1907-8, Dickie made a trip to Jerusalem, and evidently had the opportunity to visit Petra at this time. His unusual panorama format photographs of the site are extremely atmospheric, often with particularly effective use of the dramatic light to enhance the sense of discovery and adventure.

DUMAS, Tancrede R. (d.1905, active late 1860s-90s)

T.R. Dumas is something of a mystery. He was a professional photographer, most likely of Italian origin, and set up a studio in Beirut at almost the same time as Felix Bonfils, in 1867, and on the same street. As a photographer, Dumas seems to have varied enormously in the quality of his work, from the truly masterful to the downright dreadful, and even plagiaristic, suggesting a distinctly erratic character (Perez 1988: 160). Fortunately for the APES, his work as photographer, on their expedition to Eastern Palestine in 1875, counts among his finest ever produced, and indeed, the photographs are undoubtedly some of the most striking images in the PEF's collection, with bold compositions, and a number of stunning panoramas. The vast majority of the Dumas photographs in the PEF's collections are albumen paper prints from the APES survey.

GERMER-DURAND, J. (1845-1917)

Father Joseph Germer-Durand, of the Assumptionist Fathers, was an epigrapher and a self-taught archaeologist, who specialized in particular in the Roman period. The Assumptionist Fathers of Notre Dame appear to have had a singularly important role in the development of scientific architectural and archaeological photography, and Germer-Durand appears to have been influential in this area as well. He travelled widely throughout the Levant, and took numerous photographs of sites in Transjordan, Palestine, Lebanon, and Syria. Many of these are now housed in the extensive collections of the École Biblique in Jerusalem.[6]

GOOD, Frank Mason (active in Near East 1866-75)

Frank Mason Good was a British photographer who was active in the Near East during the 1860 and 1870s. His early work was associated with that of the highly successful photographer, Francis Frith, who published a number of his photographs as part of his own series, including all those published here (Perez 1988: 169). Good made a total of four trips to Palestine, from 1866 to 1875 (Gibson 2003: 175), and it was during his first trip, in the winter of 1866-7, that his astonishing pictures of Petra and the Edomite landscape were taken. Good's photographs stand out as fine examples of the best large format photographs, with extraordinary depth of field and sharpness of detail. The PEF's collection of albumen paper prints by F.M. Good have been donated to the archive by a number of individuals over the years.

HORNSTEIN, Charles Alexander (active 1895-1920)

Charles Alexander Hornstein was a native of Jerusalem, the son of German-Jewish immigrants who converted to Christianity. The Hornsteins were among the foremost hoteliers in Jerusalem. Charles' uncle, Moses Hornstein, ran the famous Mediterranean Hotel, and from the 1870s, his father, Aaron, was the proprietor of the Hotel de l'Europe (also known as the Damascus Hotel). Both establishments courted British and American custom, and had strong connections with Thomas Cook & Son. The two hotels worked as a partnership, with the Hôtel de l'Europe acting as an annex to the nearby Mediterranean when it reached capacity. The Mediterranean was the hotel of choice for, among others, the PEF explorers, and so it is entirely plausible that the young Hornstein would have grown up very familiar with the exploits of the various expeditions that used the hotels as their base. Hornstein became Principal of the London Jews Society/Bishop Gobat's Boy's School, and photographer for the Anglican Church in Jerusalem from 1902 to 1920 (Gibson & Chapman 1995: 93-105). He gave 23 photographs (gelatine prints) from his trip to Transjordan to the PEF in 1896.[7] A selection of these was published, with an accompanying article, in the April 1898 edition of the *Quarterly Statement*.

Hornstein's photographs of Transjordan indicate his broad interests. Not only was he concerned with recording the architectural and archaeological heritage of the country, but also its people, and their way of life. He was not unique in this. Many photographers, including some of those employed by the PEF and other expeditions, were as concerned with 'manners and customs' as with the buildings and landscape, but very few seem to have translated this to the people of Transjordan. As well as being invaluable from this perspective, Hornstein's photographs are often of a very high technical and aesthetic standard. He developed a strong sense of composition, which he often used to dramatic effect.

HULL, E. Gordon (active 1883-4)

Son of the geologist, Professor Edward Hull, Dr. E. Gordon Hull was a medical doctor by training. He acted as medical officer and photographer on the PEF's survey of the Wadi Arabah in the winter of 1883-4, along with his father, and Captain H. H. Kitchener. Evidently, Gordon Hull experienced some difficulties in his role as photographer. The gelatine prints of the Sinai and Wadi Arabah in the PEF's collection are almost all underexposed, and were never published as a group, nor were copies put on sale by the Fund. A note, scribbled on the front page of the album containing the prints, describes them as, 'Worthless – some of them would do for block illustrations'. This is indeed what happened to the photographs, which were used as the basis for the illustrations in Edward Hull's popular account of the survey, *Mount Seir, Sinai and Western Palestine*. Subsequently, an occasional image from the set has been published, but the current volume is the first time that a substantial group of the images has been seen together.

KITCHENER, Horatio H. (1850-1916)

Kitchener, (later Earl Kitchener of Khartoum), is best known as the ultimate Victorian military hero, and iconic face of the recruitment campaign of the First World War. However, in his early career, as a relatively harmless young Lieutenant in the Royal Engineers straight out of Chatham, he was employed by the PEF as a surveyor and photographer, first under C.R. Conder on the Survey of Western Palestine (and from 1877-8 as field leader), and then as part of the team (minus the camera) on the Wadi Arabah Survey of 1883-4. His photographs from the Survey of Western Palestine display a greater talent for detailed, close-up subjects than for open landscapes. Many of his most successful images focus on a specific architectural detail, where he had an ability to create striking, almost abstract, geometric compositions out of the strong shapes of crumbling arches, or wooden scaffolding frames surrounding a structure. He was also fond of including a human figure, often reclining, as a scale, or to give 'human interest' in a slightly romantic, and very Victorian (though not military) style. The portrait of Claude Conder at Jericho (Fig 16, Chapter 1) is a prime example of this type.

LAWRENCE, Thomas Edward (1888-1935)

T.E. Lawrence was another PEF explorer made world famous by his later military exploits. Before he became 'Lawrence of Arabia', T.E. Lawrence was a budding archaeology student, with an archaeology degree from Oxford, a find dissertation on Syrian Crusader castles, and digging experience in Egypt with Sir William Flinders Petrie under his belt. At the time of his employment by the PEF, he was assistant to Leonard Woolley (yet another man who later found greatness, this time within the world of archaeology) at the British Museum's excavations in Carchemish in northern Syria. The photographs from the Wilderness of Zin survey were taken by both Woolley and Lawrence. On analysis, it transpires that those images in the PEF's archives taken on nitrate film correspond to Woolley's route after the pair split, and those on glass plate negatives to Lawrence's. It has, therefore, been possible to determine which photographs were taken by which man (Gibson & Chapman 1996: 99-102). As photographs, Lawrence's images are often striking, utilizing where possible the strong light of the desert. However, the trying physical conditions of the desert have also taken their toll on the delicate materials of the photographs, sometimes producing strange patterns of shadow, or leaving specks of dust and detritus sticking to the emulsion on the glass plate negative.

McDONALD, James (active in Near East 1864-5, & 1868-9)

Sergeant James McDonald, R.E. was one of the most exceptional photographers working in the Near East. His views of Jerusalem, published in the *Ordnance Survey of Jerusalem* in 1865, are among the most impressive ever taken of this most photographed of cities. He worked again as photographer in the Sinai in 1868-9, and his photographs of this epic landscape are truly stunning. After this date, he became manager of the Photographic Office of the Royal Engineer's Establishment in Chatham (Perez 1988: 197-8).

MACKENZIE, Duncan & NEWTON, Francis G. (active in Near East 1909-1913)

Mackenzie and Newton were employed by the PEF from 1909 to 1912 to excavate the site of 'Ain Shems (the biblical Beth-Shemesh), west of Jerusalem. However, the relationship between the two men (particularly Mackenzie), and their employers, was not always a happy one, due to a combination of personality clashes, misunderstandings, and lack of efficiency (both with money and reports) on the part of the employees. The pair's excursion to Petra and Transjordan was the first instance in which they quarrelled with the PEF. Whilst waiting for the necessary paperwork and official Ottoman personnel to begin their excavations at 'Ain Shems, Mackenzie and Newton decided to make use of their time to visit Petra. However, they failed to acquire the necessary permission from the Ottoman authorities, which angered both them, and the Committee of the PEF, who were put in an awkward position. Mackenzie was somewhat surprised by the reaction of the PEF, to what he saw as a valuable use of their time, and the PEF's money (Momigliano 1996: 139-170).

Both Mackenzie and Newton seem to have taken photographs during the excavations at 'Ain Shems, and on their excursions into Palestine and Syria as a whole. Not all the images have survived the ravages of time as well as other photographs in this book, but even so, many have an immediate, journalistic quality that is refreshing. In addition, their photographs from Petra and Transjordan are important as records of the many monuments now lost, and of a landscape and way of life that was also fast disappearing.

MANTELL, A. M. (active in Near East 1881-2)

Lieutenant Mantell, R.E. was employed by the PEF as surveyor and photographer on the Survey of Eastern Palestine under the direction of Captain Claude R. Conder. His photographs from this expedition formed the basis for many of the sketch drawings that illustrated the final volume of the *Survey of Eastern Palestine* published in 1898. After the survey, Mantell became a member of the PEF's General Committee (Hodson 1999: 65)

At a Meeting of the PEF held in November 1880, the subject of the proposed Eastern Survey was very much on the agenda. Lieutenant Conder publicly accepted the leadership of the expedition, and expressed high hopes for the success of the venture. The Dean of Westminster was also very enthusiastic about the survey as a whole. Regarding the photographs, he had a very particular point of view: 'There is one remark I should like to make about the photographs. All the photographs of Palestine should be invariably photographs of buildings and of ruins; photographs of landscapes appear to me always nearly worthless. I beg Lieutenant Conder if he has any influence over the photographer who is with him, to induce him to spend all his efforts upon the buildings, and none on the landscape.' (Besant (?) 1881: 25). Whatever the virtues or otherwise of this statement, Mantell's photographs do focus primarily on architecture and ruins. However, they are also a valuable source of images of the local tribesmen who accompanied them, under the leadership of their sheikh, Gublan, and it is for this as much as for their value as a record of Jordan's antiquities that they are to be noted today.

PHILLIPS, Henry (1830s-1905/6)

Corporal Henry Phillips R.E. was perhaps the single most important photographer who worked directly for the PEF. During the course of two expeditions (the first with Captain Wilson in 1865-66, and the second with Lieutenant Charles Warren in 1867-69), he made nearly 370 glass plate negatives for the PEF, of which 349 survive in the Fund's collections. The photographs in this volume come from the later, Warren expedition, during which the team made several forays into the countryside of Palestine, the Jordan Valley, and Transjordan. By comparison with the published accounts of these trips in the *Quarterly Statements*,[8] and in the PEF's archives, it has been possible to date many of the photographs extremely accurately, sometimes even to the time of day they were taken. On leaving the Royal Engineers, in 1874, Phillips set up a photographic studio in Farnborough, Surrey, a town with many army connections (Gibson 2003: 183-4).

Phillips' photographs are generally of a very high technical standard, although sometimes the harsh conditions of the environment got the better of his equipment and chemicals. He shows a fine eye for detail, and for composition, and he was very much at home with the broad, sweeping landscapes of Transjordan, capturing the sense of space and isolation most effectively.

PHOTOCHROM (PHOTOGLOB) COMPANY (1880s onwards)

This company, based in Zurich, Switzerland, produced hugely popular colour tinted prints of scenes from the Eastern Mediterranean, which were sold well into the 1930s. The company used a chemical process, known as photochrome, or photochromy, to tint artificially existing photographic prints, by mechanically applying layers of colour, one at a time (Coe & Haworth-Booth: 104). Many of the images were Bonfils originals, but the extraordinary coloration gives the photographs an entirely different character.

REID, A. (active in Near East 1914-1920s)

Surprisingly little is known about this photographer, despite his obvious skill and access to important personages such as Emir Abdullah. The PEF photographic collection contains 14 glass plate negatives, and 15 silver gelatine prints, possibly all taken by Reid. Some prints are stamped with the legend 'A. Reid FCI (England, Central News, P.O.B. 1481 (Cairo, Egypt).' They contain images from Egypt and the Western Desert, Palestine, and Syria, and some are of an official nature, or show officials such as British soldiers and Syrian policemen engaged in activities. The three photographs of Emir Abdullah and his entourage are the most striking of all the images taken. The quality of the photography is extremely high, adding hugely to their value as historical records.

RHODES, Arthur (1892-1922)

Captain Arthur Rhodes was a New Zealander, and a soldier in the Beersheba Campaign of the First World War. He served in Egypt in the staff of Major General Chaytor of the ANZAC Divisions, acting as his ADC. After the War, he spent a brief spell in France before returning home to South Canterbury in New Zealand. He died just a few years later, at the tragically young age of 30. His daughter, Anne Scarlett, donated a collection of his photographs to the PEF in 1996. Rhodes' photographs of the War in the Levant combine a great journalistic sense with a keen aesthetic appreciation, and he was clearly a photographer of considerable skill.

SMITH, John Shaw (1811-1873)

John Shaw Smith was an Irishman of independent means, which enabled him to devote a substantial amount of time and money to his passion in life – the new discipline of photography. A member of the Dublin Photographic Society, he was one of the earliest people to take photographs in the southern Levant, and was certainly a true pioneer east of the River Jordan. His images of Petra were taken during a trip he made with his wife to the Orient, covering Egypt, Palestine, Lebanon, Syria, and Transjordan (Perez 1988: 222). The PEF received a collection of 38 gelatine silver prints made in 1906 from the original negatives, from his daughter, Annie Smith, the donation of which is recorded in the minutes of the PEF for the December of that year.[9]

John Shaw Smith's photographs are unmistakable, often with a noticeable texture that adds to the atmosphere of the dramatic landscapes of his photographs. Given their early date, and the remote and difficult locations he was working in, his photographs are extraordinary technical and artistic achievements.

NOTES

1. In the Calotype process, the image was exposed on paper, as glass plates were not yet available. The process was complex and cumbersome, and required a very long exposure time (7-15 minutes) which could mean a disappointing result, and a limit to what could be effectively photographed. The exposed paper was then coated in wax to make it translucent. Prints were made from the negative by pressing a piece of sensitized paper to the negative, and directing a light source through the negative to the paper to produce a Salt Print.

2. Frederick Scott Archer discovered that a negative image could be created by coating a glass plate in a solution of collodion (nitrocellulose dissolved in ether and alcohol) and the light-sensitive agents of potassium iodide and silver nitrate. The glass plate was more transparent than the waxed paper of the Calotype method, producing far more detailed images. A positive print was achieved using the same principle as that of the Calotype/Salt Print method, namely, by making a 'shadow' on pre-treated paper by passing a light source through the negative onto the surface of the paper. However, the medium most commonly used was now albumen coated paper, treated with silver-nitrate, which produced far finer results than were possible on a salt print. The positive image had to be developed before the emulsion had dried, making it necessary to have a dark room immediately to hand after the exposure had been taken. Working in the hot, dry, and inhospitable country of the southern Levant, one can imagine how difficult this would have been to achieve successfully. The photographers, particularly those working in the earlier decades covered by this volume, would have had to transport, along with everything else, a make-shift dark room (often a black canvas tent), with all their developing chemicals and equipment. Despite the difficulties attached to this technique, it had the advantage of requiring significantly less exposure time; perhaps only three minutes in contrast to the 15 of the Calotype method.

3. The Gelatine Dry Plate process replaced the wet collodian solution with one that employed gelatine as the binding agent. The key factors in this advance were that it was possible to allow the solution to dry before developing, and it generally required even shorter exposure times when taking the photograph than the wet collodian process had done previously.

4. PEF/DA/EC/ PEF Minute Book 5: Minutes from meeting of PEF Executive Committee held 17 October, 1899.

5. PEF/EC/ PEF/Minute Book 5: Minutes from meeting of PEF Executive Committee held 5 March 1895.

6. See http://ebaf.op.org/photoq/fr/trimbur.html#n8 for an article by Jean-Michel de Tarragon, OP on the role of the Assumptionist Fathers in the development of archaeological photography in Palestine.

7. PEF/DA/EC/ PEF Minute Book 5: Minute from Meeting of PEF Executive Committee held May 5 1896.

8. See the numerous reports on the trips to Transjordan and elsewhere in the Levant by Charles Warren in *the Palestine Exploration Quarterly Statements* for the years 1869-1872.

9. PEF/DA/EC/ PEF Minute Book 6: Minutes of Meeting of PEF Executive Committee held on 4 December 1906.

Appendix II

List of Illustrations

CHAPTER 1
Fig 1: G Armstrong,. 1894. (PEF/P/SWP/Relief Map)
Fig 2: J. MacGregor. 1869 (PEF/DA/MACG/1/36)
Fig 3: H. Salt. 1817 (Frontispiece, *Travels in Syria and the Holy Land*, London 1822).
Fig 4: W. T. Fry. (Frontispiece, *Travels in Palestine* London 1821)
Fig 5: Frontispiece, *Journey though Arabia Petraea* London 1836
Fig 6: C. R. Conder. *Palestine* London 1889. P.16)
Fig 7: Charles Laurie. Published London & Edinburgh, 1882 (PEF/PORTRAIT/Stanley)
Fig 8: H. H. Phillips. August 1867. (PEF/P/1315)
Fig 9:, J. MacGregor. 1869 (PEF/DA/MACG/1/34)
Fig 10: J. MacDonald. (PEF/P/SIN/Survey Team)
Fig 11: Maull & Fox. London. No date. (PEF/PORTRAIT/Tristram)
Fig 12: C. Warren & E.H.Palmer, et al. New York 1872 (in the private collection of RSA)
Fig 13: T. R. Dumas. 1875 APES No. 75. (Courtesy of the Fine Arts Library, Harvard College Library, Boston)
Fig 14: R. Meyer & Ordnance Survey. 1879 (PEF/M/APES/Key Map)
Fig 15: O Schoefft. No date. (PEF/PORTRAIT/Mantell)
Fig 16: H. H. Kitchener. 1874-5 (PEF/P/3574)
Fig 17: E. G. Hull. 1883-4 (PEF/P/4195)
Fig 18: H. H. Kitchener, G. Armstrong, & E. Hull. 1883-4 & Stanfords. No date. (PEF/M/ARABAH/6)
Fig 19: C. R. Conder & A. M Mantell 1881 & Stanfords. No date. (PEF/M/ES/Eastern Survey Map)
Fig 20: F. G. Newton. 1911. (PEF/P/MACK/218)
Fig 21: F Weston. No date. (PEF/PORTRAIT/Bliss)
Fig 22: D. Mackenzie / F. G. Newton. 1912. (PEF/P/MACK/345)

CHAPTER 2
Fig 23: F. Cobbing. 2004
Fig 24: Fr. A. Klein. 1868. (PEF/DA/Klein)
Fig 25: H.H. Kitchener. 1874. (PEF/DA/WS/KIT/83)

CHAPTER 3
Fig 26:. E. G. Hull. 1883-4. (PEF/P/4196)
Fig 27: E. G. Hull. 1883-4. (PEF/P/4190)
Fig 28: E. G. Hull. 1883-4 (PEF/P/4206)
Fig 29: E. G. Hull. 1883-4 (PEF/P/4228)
Fig 30: E. G. Hull. 1883-4 (PEF/P/4229)
Fig 31: E. G. Hull. 1883 (PEF/P/4208)
Fig 32: E. G. Hull 1883-4 (PEF/P/4231)
Fig 33: E. G. Hull. 1883-4. (PEF/P/4175)
Fig 34: E. G. Hull. 1883-4. (PEF/P/4176)
Fig 35: E. G. Hull. 1883-4. (PEF/P/4215)
Fig 36: E. G. Hull. 1883-4. (PEF/P/4216)
Fig 37: E. G. Hull. 1883-4. (PEF/P/4197)
Fig 38: E .G. Hull. 1883-4. (PEF/P/4210)

Fig 39: E. G. Hull. 1883-4. (PEF/P/4188)
Fig 40: Photochrom Co. 1880 – 1900. Photochrom No. 15,050 P.Z. (PEF/P/2632)
Fig 41: C.R. Conder 1873. (PEF/PI/113)
Fig 42:. Bonfils. 1867-96. Bonfils No. 910. (PEF/P/1898)
Fig 43: Bonfils. 1867-96. Bonfils No. 341. (PEF/P/1863)
Fig 44: Photochrom Co. 1880 – 1900. Photochrom No. 15,121 P.Z. (PEF/P/2667)
Fig 45: H. Phillips. July 1867. (PEF/P/1119)
Fig 46: D. Mackenzie / F.G. Newton. 1911 (PEF/P/MACK/Loose prints – R. Jordan Bridge)
Fig 47: Photochrom Co. 1880 – 1900. Photochrom No. 15,051 P.Z (PEF/P/2633)
Fig 48: H. Phillips. 1867. (PEF/P/893)
Fig 49: H. Phillips. 1867. (PEF/P/891)

CHAPTER 4
Fig 50: C Warren et al. 1867. (PEF/DA/JER/WAR/61/7/3)
Fig 51: G. Schumacher. 1886 (PEF/M/SCHUM/103)
Fig 52: G. Schumacher. 1886. (PEF/DA/SCHUM/93a/p53)
Fig 53: T. R. Dumas. 1875. APES No. 47 (PEF/P/1679)
Fig 54: T. R. Dumas. 1875. APES No. 48. (PEF/P/1680)
Fig 55: H. Phillips. 1867. (PEF/P/1278)
Fig 56:. T. R. Dumas. 1875. APES No. 70 (PEF/P/1694)
Fig 57: T.R. Dumas. 1875. APES No. 52 - 53 (Panorama runs from No. 49-55) (PEF/P/1684-5)
Fig 58: H. Phillips. 1867. (PEF/P/1270)
Fig 59: T. R. Dumas. 1875. APES No. 49. (PEF/P/1681)
Fig 60: T. R. Dumas. 1875. APES No. 51. (PEF/P/1683)
Fig 61: T. R. Dumas. 1875. APES No. 58. (PEF/P/1688)
Fig 62: H. Phillips. 1867. (PEF/P/1290)
Fig 63: H. Phillips. 1867. (PEF/P/1317)
Fig 64: T.R. Dumas. 1875. APES No. 54 (PEF/P/1686)
Fig 65: H. Phillips. 1867. (PEF/P/1286)
Fig 66: H. Phillips. 1867. (PEF/P/1274)
Fig 67: T. .R. Dumas. 1875. APES No. 55. (PEF/P/1687)
Fig 68: H. Phillips. 1867. (PEF/P/1282)
Fig 69: T. R. Dumas. 1875. APES No. 61. (PEF/P/1690)
Fig 70: H. Phillips. 1867. (PEF/P/1256)
Fig 71: T. R. Dumas. 1875. APES No. 66. (PEF/P/1692)
Fig 72: H. Phillips. 1867. (PEF/P/1260)
Fig 73: H. Phillips. 1867. (PEF/P/1293)
Fig 74: H. Phillips. 1867. (PEF/P/1265)
Fig 75: T. R. Dumas. 1875. APES No. 68. (PEF/P/1693)
Fig 76:. H. Phillips. 1867. (PEF/P/1250)
Fig 77: T. .R. Dumas. 1875. APES No. 49 – 55. (P1861 – 1867)

CHAPTER 5
Fig 78: H. Phillips. 1867. (PEF/P/1208)
Fig 79: H. Phillips. 1867. (PEF/P/1203)
Fig 80: A.M. Mantell. 1881. (PEF/P/4048)
Fig 81: D. Mackenzie / F.G. Newton. 1910. (PEF/P/MACK/17)
Fig 82. D. Mackenzie / F.G. Newton. 1910. (PEF/P/MACK/25)
Fig 83: D. Mackenzie / F.G. Newton. 1910. (PEF/P/MACK/24)
Fig 84: A. M. Mantell. 1881. (PEF/P/4086)
Fig 85 .D. Mackenzie / F.G. Newton. 1910. (PEF/P/MACK/20)
Fig 86: D. Mackenzie / F.G. Newton. 1910. (PEF/P/MACK/18)
Fig 87: D. Mackenzie / F.G. Newton. 1910 (PEF/P/MACK/23)
Fig 88: T. R. Dumas. 1875. APES No. 89 – 94 (PEF/P/1707–10)

Fig 89: C. Warren et al. 1867. (PEF/DA/JER/WAR/61/8)
Fig 90: H. Phillips. 1867. (PEF/P/1181)
Fig 91: H. Phillips. 1867. (PEF/P/1219)
Fig 92: H. Phillips. 1867. (PEF/P/1190)
Fig 93: H. Phillips. 1867. (PEF/P/1194)
Fig 94: A. M. Mantell. 1881. (PEF/P/4120)
Fig 95: A.M. Mantell. 1881. (PEF/P/4134)
Fig 96: H. Phillips. 1867. (PEF/P/1216)
Fig 97: A.M. Mantell. 1881. (PEF/P/4056)
Fig 98: H. Phillips. 1867. (PEF/P/1227)
Fig 99: A.M. Mantell 1881. (PEF/P/4136)
Fig 100: A.M. Mantell. 1881. (PEF/P/4046)
Fig 101: D. Mackenzie / F. G. Newton. 1910. (PEF/P/MACK/14)
Fig 102: D. Mackenzie / F. G. Newton. 1910. (PEF/P/MACK/16)
Fig 103: D. Mackenzie / F. G. Newton. 1910. (PEF/P/MACK/10)
Fig 104: D. Mackenzie / F. G. Newton. 1910. (PEF/P/MACK/Theatre, Amman)
Fig 105: Mackenzie/F. G. Newton. 1910. (PEF/P/MACK/9)
Fig 106: A.M. Mantell. 1881. (PEF/P/4062)
Fig 107: A.M. Mantell. 1881. (PEF/P/4063)
Fig 108: A.M. Mantell. 1881 (PEF/P/1180)
Fig 109: A.M. Mantell. 1881. (PEF/P/4057)
Fig 110: A.M. Mantell. 1881. (PEF/P/4054)
Fig 111: H. Phillips. 1867. (PEF/P/1303)
Fig 112: H. Phillips. 1867. (PEF/P/1306/1311)
Fig 113: T. R. Dumas. 1875. APES No. 72 - 73. (PEF/P/1695-6)
Fig 114: T. R. Dumas. 1875. APES No. 74. (PEF/P/1697)
Fig 115: J. Clark. 1897. (PEF/ PI/40)
Fig 116: H. Phillips. 1867. (PEF/P/1171)
Fig 117: H. Phillips. 1867. (PEF/P/1174)
Fig 118: H. Phillips. 1867. (PEF/P/1166)
Fig 119: T. R. Dumas. 1875. APES No. 78. (PEF/P/1700)
Fig 120: T. R. Dumas. 1875. APES No. 79. (PEF/P/1701)
Fig 121: H. Phillips. 1867. (PEF/P/1134)
Fig 122: H. Phillips. 1867. (PEF/P/1147)
Fig 123: T. R. Dumas. 1875. APES No. 76-77 (PEF/P/1698-99)
Fig 124: A. M. Mantell. 1881. (PEF/P/4079)
Fig 125: A. M. Mantell. 1881. (PEF/P/4080)
Fig 126: A. M. Mantell. 1881. (PEF/P/4082)
Fig 127: A .M. Mantell. 1881. (PEF/P/4081)
Fig 128: A. M. Mantell. 1881. (PEF/P/4090)

CHAPTER 6
Fig 129: C.A. Hornstein. 1895. (PEF/P/2408)
Fig 130: C.A. Hornstein. 1895. (PEF/P/2400)
Fig 131: F .J. Bliss. 1895. (PEF/P/1923)
Fig 132: Fr. J. Germer-Durand. 1897. (PEF/P/BLISS/Mosaic Map Composit)
Fig 133: F. J. Bliss. 1895. (PEF/P/1917)
Fig 134:. C. A. Hornstein. 1895. (PEF/P/2402)
Fig 135:. C. A. Hornstein. 1895. (PEF/P/2303)
Fig 136: T. R. Dumas. 1875. APES 'No. 87 (PEF/P/1705)
Fig 137: T. R. Dumas. 1875. APES 'No. 88 (PEF/P/1706)
Fig 138: F .J. Bliss. 1895. (PEF/P/1918)
Fig 139: H. Phillips. 1867. (PEF/P/1158)
Fig 140: H. Phillips. 1867. (PEF/P/1153)
Fig 141: C. A. Hornstein. 1895. (PEF/P2340)
Fig 142: C. A. Hornstein. 1895. (PEF/P/2423)
Fig 143: C. A. Hornstein. 1895. (PEF/P/2403)
Fig 144: D. Mackenzie / F. G. Newton. 1910. (PEF/P/MACK/33)
Fig 145: F. J. Bliss. 1895. (PEF/P/1924)

APPENDIX II

Fig 146: C. A. Hornstein. 1895. (PEF/P/2367)
Fig 147: D. Mackenzie / F. G. Newton. 1910. (PEF/P/MACK/41)
Fig 148: PEF / unknown. c. 1870. (PEF/P/Mesha Stela)

CHAPTER 7
Fig 149: C. A. Hornstein. 1895. (PEF/P/2364)
Fig 150: C. A. Hornstein. 1895. (PEF/P/2467)
Fig 151: F. J. Bliss. 1895. (PEF/P/1920)
Fig 152: F .J. Bliss. 1895. (PEF/P/1921)
Fig 153: F .J. Bliss. (PEF/P/2399)
Fig 154: D. Mackenzie / F. G. Newton. 1910. (PEF/P/MACK/45)
Fig 155: D.Mackenzie / F. G. Newton. 1910. (PEF/P/MACK/44)
Fig 156: D.Mackenzie / F. G. Newton. 1910. (PEF/P/MACK/46)
Fig 157: D.Mackenzie / F. G. Newton. 1910. (PEF/P/MACK/47)
Fig 158: .Mackenzie / F. G. Newton. 1910. (PEF/P/MACK/48)
Fig 159: D. Mackenzie / F. G. Newton. 1910 (PEF/P/MACK/49)
Fig 160: C. A. Hornstein. 1895. (PEF/P/2357)
Fig 161: C. A. Hornstein. 1895. (PEF/P/2360)
Fig 162: C. A. Hornstein. 1895. (PEF/P/2398)
Fig 163: C. A. Hornstein. 1895. (PEF/P/2410)
Fig 164: F. .J. Bliss. 1895. (PEF/P/1922)
Fig 165: C. A. Hornstein. 1895. (PEF/P/2296)
Fig 166: C. A. Hornstein. 1895 (PEF/P/2287)
Fig 167: C. A. Hornstein. 1895. (PEF/P/2290)
Fig 168: C. A. Hornstein. 1895. (PEF/P/2413)
Fig 169: C. A. Hornstein. 1895. (PEF/P/2412)
Fig 170: C. A. Hornstein. 1895. (PEF/P/2292)
Fig 171: C. A. Hornstein. 1895. (PEF/P/2299)
Fig 172: C. A. Hornstein. 1895. (PEF/P/2282)
Fig 173: C .A. Hornstein. (PEF/P/2307)

CHAPTER 8
Fig 174: C. A. Hornstein. 1895. (PEF/P/2373)
Fig 175: C. A.Hornstein. 1895. (PEF/P/2333)
Fig 176: C. A. Hornstein. 1895. (PEF/P/2419)
Fig 177:. D. Mackenzie / F.G. Newton. 1910. (PEF/P/MACK/72)
Fig 178: D. Mackenzie / F.G. Newton. 1910. (PEF/P/MACK/73)
Fig 179: C. A. Hornstein. 1895. (PEF/P/2310)
Fig 180: C. A. Hornstein. 1895. (PEF/P/2421)
Fig 181: C. A. Hornstein. 1895. (PEF/P/2314)
Fig 182: F.M. Good. 1866-7. Frith Series No. 543. (PEF/P/2035)
Fig 183: C. A. Hornstein. 1895. (PEF/P/2337)
Fig 184: C. A. Hornstein. 1895. (PEF//P2456)
Fig 185: C. A. Hornstein. 1895. (PEF/P/2439)
Fig 186: C. A. Hornstein. 1895. (PEF/P/2440)
Fig 187: C. A. Hornstein. 1895. (PEF/P/2458)
Fig 188: C. A. Hornstein. 1895. (PEF/P/2436)
Fig 189: L. Laborde & Linat. (Libby & Hoskins, 1905).
Fig 190: C. A. Hornstein. 1895. (PEF/P/2446)
Fig 191: D. Mackenzie / F. G. Newton. 1910. (PEF/P/MACK/53)
Fig 192: F.M. Good. 1866 -7. Frith Series No. 546. (PEF/P/2036)
Fig 193: C. A. Hornstein. 1895. (PEF/P/2424)
Fig 194: A. C. Dickie. 1907. (PEF/P/DICKIE/3)
Fig 195: C. A. Hornstein. 1895. (PEF/P/2376)
Fig 196: C. A. Hornstein. (PEF/P/2430)
Fig 197: D. Mackenzie / F.G. Newton. 1910. (PEF/P/MACK/56)
Fig 198: C. A. Hornstein. 1895. (PEF/P/2379)
Fig 199: D. Mackenzie. 1910. (PEF/P/MACK/55)
Fig 200: D. Mackenzie. 1910. (PEF/P/MACK/58)
Fig 201: D. Mackenzie. 1910 (PEF/P/MACK59)

Fig 202: F. G. Newton. 1910. (PEF/P/MACK/61)
Fig 203: A. C. Dickie. 1907. (PEF/P/DICKIE/13)
Fig 204: D. Mackenzie / F. G. Newton. 1910. (PEF/P/MACK/71)
Fig 205: J. S. Smith. 1852. (PEF/P/2557)
Fig 206: C. A. Hornstein. 1895. (PEF/P/2453)
Fig 207: J. S. Smith. 1852. (PEF/P/2554)
Fig 208: D. Mackenzie / F. G. Newton. 1910. (PEF/P/MACK/66)
Fig 209: D. Mackenzie / F. G. Newton. 1910. (PEF/P/MACK/X.1)
Fig 210: D. Mackenzie / F.G. Newton. 1910. (PEF/P/MACK/X.2)
Fig 211: C. A. Hornstein. 1895. (PEF/P/2445)
Fig 212: J. S. Smith. 1852. (PEF/P/2553)
Fig 213: J. S. Smith. 1852. (PEF/P/2552)
Fig 214: C. A. Hornstein. 1895. (PEF/P/2438)
Fig 215: C. A. Hornstein. 1895. (PEF/P/2451)
Fig 216: C. A. Hornstein. 1895. (PEF/P/2381)
Fig 217: D. Mackenzie / F. G. Newton. 1910. (PEF/P/MACK/68)
Fig 218: D. Mackenzie / F. G. Newton. 1910. (PEF/P/MACK/67)
Fig 219: J. S. Smith. 1852. (PEF/P/2556)
Fig 220: C. A. Hornstein. 1895. (PEF/P/2450)
Fig 221: F. M. Good. 1866 – 7. Frith Series No. 557 (PEF/P/2038)
Fig 222: G. Armstrong & H. H. Kitchener. 1883-4. (PEF/M/ARABAH/10)
Fig 223: C. A. Hornstein. 1895. (PEF/P/2318)
Fig 224: C. A. Hornstein. 1895. (PEF/P/2465)
Fig 225: C. A. Hornstein. (PEF/P/2320)
Fig 226: C. A. Hornstein. 1895. (PEF/P/2326)

CHAPTER 9
Fig 227: T. E. Lawrence. 1914. *Wilderness of Zin,* 2003, Pl. III.II. (PEF/P/W-L/6)
Fig 228: A Reid. 1914. (PEF/P/REID/12)
Fig 229:, T.E. Lawrence. 1914. *Wilderness of Zin* 2003 Pl. III.1 (PEF/P/W-L/5)
Fig 230: E. G. Hull. 1883. (PEF/P/4177)
Fig 231: E. G. Hull. 1883. (PEF/P/4178)
Fig 232: E. G. Hull. 1883. (PEF/P/4179)
Fig 233: A. Rhodes. 1918. (PEF/P/RHODES/126)
Fig 234: A. Rhodes. 1918. (PEF/P/RHODES/165)
Fig 235: A Rhodes. 1917. (PEF/P/RHODES/166)
Fig 236: A. Rhodes. 1918. (PEF/P/RHODES/164)
Fig 237: A. Rhodes. 1918. (PEF/P/RHODES/129)
Fig 238: A. Rhodes. 1918. (PEF/P/RHODES/122)
Fig 239: A. Rhodes. 1918. (PEF/P/RHODES/156)
Fig 240: A. Rhodes. 1918. (PEF/P/RHODES/163)
Fig 241: A. Rhodes. 1918. (PEF/P/RHODES/125)
Fig 242: A. Reid. 1921. (PEF/P/REID/18)
Fig 243: A. Reid. 1921. (PEF/P/REID/7)

Bibliography

Abujaber, R. S., *Pioneers over Jordan*. London. 1989.
Al-Abidi, M., *Islamic Sites in Palestine and Jordan*. Amman. 1973.
Al-Madhi, M., and Musa, S., *A History of Transjordan in the 20th Century*. Volume 1. Amman (Arabic). 1959.
Al-Muqqadasi, Mohammad bin Ahmad, *Ahsan Al-Taqasim*. Leiden. 1909.
Antonius, G., *The Arab Awakening*. London. 1938.
Bell, G. L., *The Desert and the Sown*. London. 1919
Ben-Arieh, Y. *The Rediscovery of the Holy Land in the Nineteenth Century*. Jerusalem – Detroit. 1979.
Besant, W.(?), Meeting of the Palestine Exploration Fund. Jerusalem Chamber, Westminster Abbey, Tuesday, November 30th, 1880. *Palestine Exploration Quarterly Statement* (1881): 5-26. 1881
Besant, W., *Thirty Years' Work in the Holy Land (a Record and a Summary). Published for the Committee of the Palestine Exploration Fund*. London. 1895.
bin-Mungidh, U., *Kitab Al-'Itibar* (ed. P. Hitti). Cairo. 2001.
Blakely, J., Frederick Jones Bliss. Pp.332-333 in E. M. Meyers ed., *Oxford Encyclopedia of Archaeology in the Near East*. Vol. 1. New York & Oxford. 1997.
Bliss, F. J., Narrative of an Expedition to Moab and Gilead in March 1895. *Palestine Exploration Fund Quarterly Statement* (1895): 203-235. 1895.
Blythe, E.(?), Obituary: The Late Professor A.C. Dickie. *Palestine Exploration Fund Quarterly Statement* (1942): 5-7. 1942.
Bourke, S. J., The Chalcolithic Period. Pp. 107-162 in B. MacDonald, R. Adams and P. Bienkowski (eds.), *The Archaeology of Jordan*. Sheffield. 2001.
Braemer, F. Jerash. Pp. 316-337 in D. Homès Fredericq and J. B. Hennessy (eds.), *Archaeology of Jordan II: Field Reports*. Akkadica Supplementum VII. 1989. Leuven.
Browning, I., *Jerash and the Decapolis*. London. 1982.
—— *Petra*. London. 1989.
Brunnow, R. and von Domaszewski, A., *Die Provincia Arabia*. Strasburg. 1904.
Buckingham, J. S., *Travels among the Arab Tribes Inhabiting the Countries East of Syria and Palestine*. London. 1825.
Burckhardt, J., *Travels in Syria and the Holy Land*. London. 1822.
Butler, H. C., *Ancient Architecture in Syria*. Publications of the Princeton University Archaeological Expedition to Syria, 1904-5 and 1909. (9 volumes.) Leiden. 1913.
Byrd, B. F., Beidha. Pp. 291-292 in E. M. Meyers ed., *Oxford Encyclopedia of Archaeology in the Near East*. Vol. 1. New York & Oxford. 1997.
Clermont-Ganneau, C., The Madeba Mosaic. *Palestine Exploration Fund Quarterly Statement* (1897): 213-225.
Coe, B., & Haworth-Booth, M., *A Guide to Early Photographic Processes*. London. 1983.
Conder, C. R. *The Princes' Visit to the Holy Land*. London. 1882.
—— *Heth and Moab*. London. 1885.
—— *The Survey of Western Palestine: Memoir, the Survey of Eastern Palestine*. London. 1889.
Curtiss, S. I., The High Place and Altar at Petra. *Palestine Exploration Quarterly Statement* (1900): 350-355. 1900.
Dalman, G., The Khazneh at Petra. *Palestine Exploration Fund Annual* 1: 95-107. 1911.

de Saulcy, F., *Narrative of a Journey round the Dead Sea and in the Bible Lands.* London. 1854.

de Vogue, M., *Le Temple de Jerusalem.* Paris. 1864.

De Vries, B., *Umm el-Jimal: A Tour Guide.* Amman. 1982

——— Umm el-Jimal. Pp. 276-279 in E. M. Meyers ed., *Oxford Encyclopedia of Archaeology in the Near East.* Vol. 5. New York & Oxford. 1997.

Dornemann, R., Amman. Pp. 98-102 in E. M. Meyers ed., *Oxford Encyclopedia of Archaeology in the Near East.* Vol. 1. New York & Oxford. 1997.

Doughty, C. M., *Travels in Arabia Deserta.* Cambridge. 1888.

Durley, T., *Lethaby of Moab.* London. 1910.

El-Edroos, S. A., *The Hashemite Arab Army 1908-1917: An Appreciation and Analysis of Military Operations.* Amman. 1980.

Fish, H.C., *Bible Lands Illustrated.* Connecticut. 1876.

Fisk, G., *A Pastor's Memorial of Egypt, the Red Sea, the Wilderness of Sin and Paran, Mount Sinai, Jerusalem and other Principal Localities of the Holy Land, Visited in 1842.* London. 1843.

Fromkin, D., *A Peace to End all Peace: Creating the Modern Middle East 1914-1922.* Hamondsworth. 1991.

Gibson, J. C. L., *Textbook of Syrian Semitic Inscriptions, Volume I: Hebrew and Moabite Inscriptions.* Oxford. 1971.

Gibson, S., & Chapman, R. L., The Mediterranean Hotel in Nineteenth Century Jerusalem. *Palestine Exploration Quarterly Statement* 217: 93-105. 1995.

——— A Note on T.E. Lawrence as photographer in the Wilderness of Zin. *Palestine Exploration Quarterly Statement* 218: 99-102. 1996.

Gibson, S. *Jerusalem in Original Photographs.* London. 2003.

Harding, G. L., *The Antiquities of Jordan.* London. 1959.

Herr, L. G. and Najjar, M., The Iron Age. Pp. 323-345 in B. MacDonald, R. Adams and P. Bienkowski (eds.), *The Archaeology of Jordan.* Sheffield. 2001.

Hill, G., *With the Beduins.* London. 1891.

Hodson, Y., An Introduction to the Publication of the Map and Memoirs. Pp.33-71 in Y. Hodson and D. M. Jacobson, *The Survey of Western Palestine Introductory Essays.* London. 1991.

Holm-Nielsen, S., Wagner-Lux, U., Vriezen, K. J. H. and Weber, T., Um Qeis. Pp. 597-611 in D. Homès Fredericq and J. B. Hennessy (eds.), *Archaeology of Jordan II: Field Reports.* Akkadica Supplementum VIII. Leuven. 1989.

Hornstein, C. A., A Visit to Kerak and Petra. *Palestine Exploration Fund Quarterly Statement* (1898): 94-103. 1898.

Hull, E., *Mount Seir, Sinai and Western Palestine.* London. 1885.

——— *The Survey of Western Palestine: Memoir on the Physical Geology and Geography of Arabia Petraea, Palestine, and Adjoining Districts. With Special Reference to the Mode of Formation of the Jordan-Arabah Depression and the Dead Sea.* London. 1886.

Irby, C. and Mangles, J., *Travels in Egypt & Nubia, Syria and Asia Minor during the Years 1817 and 1818.* London. 1823.

Jaussen, P. A., *Coutumes des Arabes au Pays de Moab.* Paris. 1907.

Kennedy, D., *The Roman Army in Jordan.* London. 2000.

Khalaf, M. and Haddadin, A., *'Ashai'r al-Haddadin until 1991.* Amman. 1992.

Kinglake, A. W., *Eothen.* London. 1845.

Laborde, L. de, *Journey through Arabia Petraea.* Paris. 1830.

Lawrence, T.E., *Revolt in the Desert.* London. 1927.

——— *Seven Pillars of Wisdom.* London. 1935.

Libby, W. and Hoskins, F. E., *The Jordan Valley and Petra*. London. 1905.

Lindsay, Lord, *Letters on Egypt, Edom and the Holy Land*. London. 1839.

Luke, H. and Keith-Roach, E. (eds.), *The Handbook of Palestine and Transjordan*. London. 1934.

Lynch, W.F., *Narrative of the United States Expedition to The River Jordan and the Dead Sea*. 2nd revised edition. London. 1850.

MacAdam, H. I., *Studies in History of the Roman Province of Arabia: The Northern Sector*. BAR International Series 295. Oxford. 1986, pp 241-244. 1986.

MacGregor, J., *The Rob Roy on the Jordan*. London. 1869.

Mackenzie, D., Reports from Dr Duncan Mackenzie. *Palestine Exploration Fund Quarterly Statement* 43: 8-11. 1911a.

───── The Megalithic Monuments of Rabbath Ammon at Amman. *Palestine Exploration Fund Annual* 1: 1-40. 1911b.

Macumber, P. G., Evolving Landscape and Environment in Jordan. Pp. 1-30 in B. MacDonald, R. Adams and P. Bienkowski (eds.), *The Archaeology of Jordan*. Sheffield. 2001.

Madani, O. (ed.), *The Complete Works of King Abdullah, Ibn Al-Hussein*. Beirut. (in Arabic). 1979.

Merrill, S., *East of the Jordan*. London. 1881.

Molyneaux, T. H., Expedition to the Jordan and Dead Sea. *Journal of the Royal Geographical Society, London,* (1848): 104-180. 1848.

Momigliano, N., Duncan Mackenzie and the Palestine Exploration Fund. *Palestine Exploration Quarterly Statement* 218: 139-170. 1996.

Musa, S., *A History of Transjordan in the 20th Century, 1956-1995*. Volume 2. Amman (Arabic). 1996.

Musil, A., *Arabia Petraea*. Vienna. 1907.

Northedge, A., *Studies on Roman and Islamic Amman. Vol. 1: History, Site, & Architecture*. British Academy Monographs in Archaeology Vol.3. Oxford. 1992.

Oliphant, L., *The Land of Gilead*. London. 1880.

Ottoson, M., Gilead. Pp. 405-406 in E. M. Meyers ed., *Oxford Encyclopedia of Archaeology in the Near East*. Vol. 2. New York & Oxford. 1997.

Palmer, E.H., *The Desert of the Exodus*. New York. 1872.

Parker, T. S., The Typology of Roman and Byzantine Forts and Fortresses in Jordan. Pp. 251-260 in K. 'Amr *et al.* (eds.), *Studies in the History and Archaeology of Jordan*. Volume V. Amman. 1995.

Parr, P.J., 'The Origins and Emergence of the Nabataeans', pp27-36 in G. Markoe (ed.), *Petra Rediscovered*. London. 2003.

Perez, N. N., *Focus East. Early Photography in the Near East, 1839-1885*. New York. 1988.

Peake, F. G., Lieut. Col., *Transjordan and its Tribes*. Jerusalem (Arabic). 1934.

Philip, G., Early Bronze I-III Ages. Pp. 163-232 in B. MacDonald, R. Adams and P. Bienkowski (eds.), *The Archaeology of Jordan*. Sheffield. 2001.

Piccirillo, M. and Alliata, E. (eds.), *The Madaba Map Centenary 1897*. Jerusalem. 1998.

Prag, K., A Walk in the Wadi Hesban. Palestine Exploration Quarterly 123: 48-61. 1991.

Roberts, D., *La Terre Sainte. Vues & Monuments. Avec une description historique sur chaque planche*. Bruxelles. 1843.

Robinson, E., *Biblical Researches in Palestine and in the Adjacent Regions. A Journal of Travels in the Year 1838*. Volume I. Second Edition. Boston. 1860a

───── *Biblical Researches in Palestine and in the Adjacent Regions. A Journal of Travels in the Year 1838.* Volume II. Second Edition. Boston. 1860b

Rogan, E. L., *Frontiers of the State in the Late Ottoman Empire*. Cambridge. 1999.

Schmid, S. G., The Nabataeans: Travellers between Lifestyles. Pp.367-426 in B. MacDonald, R. Adams and P. Bienkowski (eds.), *The Archaeology of Jordan*. Sheffield. 2001.
Schumacher, G., *Across the Jordan: An Exploration and Survey of Part of Hauran and Jaulan*. London. 1886.
––––– *The Jaulan*. London. 1888.
––––– *Abila, Pella and Northern Ajlun "Within the Decapolis"*. London. 1889
Seetzen, M., *Brief Account of the Countries Adjoining the Lake of Tiberias, the Jordan and the Dead Sea*. London. 1810.
––––– *Unter Mönchen und Beduinen: Reisen in Palästina und angrenzen den Ländern 1805-1807*. Vienna. 2002.
Silberman, N. A., *Digging for God and Country: Exploration, Archaeology, and the Secret Struggle for the Holy Land 1799-1917*. New York. 1982.
Smith, G. A., *The Historical Geography of the Holy Land*. 12th edition. London. 1906.
Stanley, A. P., *Syria and Palestine in Connection with their History*. London. 1856.
Taylor, J., *Petra*. London. 1993.
Tristram, H. B., *Land of Moab*. London. 1873.
Thompson, W. M., *Lebanon, Damascus and Beyond Jordan*. New York. 1886.
Velimirovic, N., *The Prologue from Orchid*. Birmingham. 1986.
Wallin, G. D., *Travels in Arabia (1845 and 1848). With Introductory Material by W. R. Mead and M. Trautz*. Cambridge. 1979.
Warren, C., Expedition to East of Jordan, July and August, 1867. *Palestine Exploration Fund Quarterly Statement* (1870): 284-311 and 381-388. 1870.
Warburton, E., *The Crescent and the Cross*. Edgewood Illustrated Edition. Philadelphia. 1888
Waterfield, G., *Layard of Nineveh*. London. 1963.
Wilson, E.L., *Scripture Lands*. London. 1891.
Woolley, C. L. and **Lawrence**, T. E., *The Wilderness of Zin*. New Edition with Additional Material. London. 2003.
Wortabet, G. M., *Syria and the Syrians; or, Turkey in the Dependencies*. Vol. 2. London. 1856.